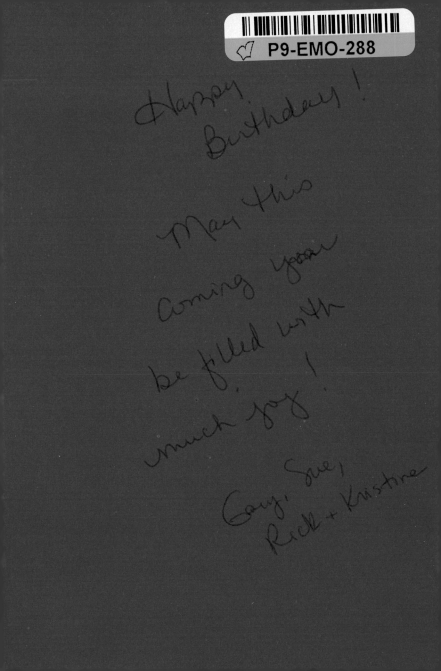

P9-EMO-288

Happy
Birthday!

May this
coming year
be filled with
much joy!

Gary, Sue,
Rick + Kristine

God's Little Devotional Book for Men

Honor Books

P.O. Box 55388

Tulsa, OK 74155

9th Printing

God's Little Devotional Book for Men
IBSN 0-56292-192-4
Copyright © 1996 by Honor Books, Inc.
P.O. Box 55388
Tulsa, Oklahoma 74155

Manuscript prepared by W. B. Freeman Concepts, Tulsa, Oklahoma.

Printed in the United States of America. All rights reserved under International Copyright Law. Contents and/or cover may not be reproduced in whole or in part in any form without the express written consent of the Publisher.

God's Little Devotional Book for Men

Presented to:

_____

Occasion:

_____

Presented by:

_____

Date:

_____

Introduction

Many people today take vitamins, attempt to eat nutritionally, and work out regularly in order to achieve and maintain physical health. The Scriptures tell us a daily "workout" of the spirit is of even greater benefit! In many ways, the book you hold in your hands can be an aid in your spiritual workout session.

As you read this book, ask the Lord to quicken the message of each devotional to your heart, and reveal how it might apply to your own life. Then, as you see ways in which the truth of God's eternal principles relate to a particular situation, problem, or opportunity that you face...*act* on what it is that you know to do, based upon God's Word!

These devotionals will open your mind, spark creative, new ideas, strengthen your spirit, and enrich your life. Then, as you allow the Lord to help you "live out" His commandments and promises on a daily basis, His Word will come alive in your heart.

We suggest you keep this book open by your nightstand or on a corner of your desk, so you can be reminded of the key quotes and Scripture references throughout the day. Educators have concluded that if a person will read aloud a verse of Scripture at least seven times a day, that verse will become a part of their active memory.

Take time to build up your inner man today!

When God measures a man, He puts the tape around the heart instead of the head.

■ ■ ■

For the Lord seeth not as man seeth;
for man looketh on the outward appearance,
but the Lord looketh on the heart.

1 Samuel 16:7

A preacher once preached an entire series of sermons on some very challenging scriptures in hopes of winning one particular man of great intellect to Christ. Shortly after the series ended, to the preacher's delight, the man came forward to announce that he had become a convinced Christian and wanted to join the church.

Pleased with himself, the preacher said, "And which of my sermons was it that removed your doubts?" The man replied, "Your sermons? It wasn't any of your sermons."

"What was it then?" the preacher asked, greatly disappointed.

The man said, "The thing that set me thinking was when a poor woman came out of the church and stumbled down the steps right beside me. When I put out my hand to help her, she smiled and said, 'Thank you' and then added, 'Do you love Jesus Christ my blessed Savior? He means everything to me.' I did not then but I thought about what she had said. I found I was on the wrong road. I still have many questions, but now Jesus means everything to me too."

Faith is not based on convincing God of our goodness. Faith is receiving God's goodness, which He has given us through Jesus Christ.

The way each day
will look to you all
starts with *who*
you're looking to.

I will lift up mine eyes unto the hills,
from whence cometh my help. My help
cometh from the Lord, which made
heaven and earth.

Psalm 121:1,2

*P*ope John Paul II has made no secret of his daily schedule in the Vatican. He begins his day at 5:30 AM, while most of Rome is asleep. By 6:15 he is in his private chapel, meditating and praying before its altar, over which hangs a large bronze crucifix. Also within sight is a copy of Poland's most cherished Catholic icon, the Black Virgin of Czestochowa.

Those who have seen the Pope in prayer state that at times he prostrates himself before the altar. At other times he sits or kneels, and with closed eyes cradles his forehead in his hands.

This early-morning prayer session is his time to bring before God his prayer requests for others. It is not uncommon for the stack of intentions to have more than 200 sheets, with many names written on each one.

The Pope considers prayer, more than liquid or food, to be the sustaining force of his life. Says Monsignor Diarmuid Martin, secretary of the Vatican's Justice and Peace Commission, the Pope makes decisions "on his knees."

Prayer...there's no better way to start a day, or to begin a decision-making process.

Live truth instead of professing it.

■　■　■

But be ye doers of the word, and not
hearers only, deceiving your own selves.

James 1:22

*D*orothy Canfield Fisher once wrote a poignant story about a physically powerful but dimwitted farm hand named Lem who lived in a Vermont valley. His mother resented him from the day he was born. She often ridiculed him with harsh and demeaning words. Even so, the boy served her till she died.

Lem was the target of village jokes. But then one night he came upon a huge dog killing some farmer's sheep. Using his bare hands as his only weapon, he strangled the dog to death. When morning came, the villagers discovered the dog was really a giant timber wolf. Lem quickly earned the villagers' silent admiration.

Later, an unwed village girl falsely accused Lem of being the father of her baby. Even though he was innocent, he married the girl so the baby would have a father. Unfortunately, the mother died within a year, so Lem raised the little girl. After she was grown and married, her own baby became desperately ill and Lem sold all his sheep to pay for the baby's medical care.

Confronted with meanness, misunderstanding, and loneliness all his life, Lem had no recourse in professing the true nature of his own life...other than to live it out in serving others. And that he did!

The loudest message you speak...is your life.

Impossibilities vanish when a man and his God confront a mountain.

...but with God all things are possible.

Matthew 19:26

When Ferdinand de Lesseps heard that his childhood friend Mohammed Said had been named viceroy of Egypt, de Lesseps wasted no time in getting to Cairo. Both men were in high spirits when they met outside Alexandria on November 13, 1854. De Lesseps had come to Egypt primarily to discuss with Said an idea he had for a canal, but he did not bring it up immediately. Instead, he waited for a sign from God. When he rose before dawn, he knew the moment had come. He later wrote: "The sun's rays were already lighting up the eastern horizon; in the west it was still dark and cloudy. Suddenly I saw a vivid-colored rainbow stretching across the sky from east to west. I must admit that I felt my heart beat violently, for...this token of a covenant...seemed to presage that the moment had come for the consummation of the Union between East and West."

De Lesseps rode immediately to Said's tent, and before the day was out, his proposal for the great Suez Canal had been approved.

God may not send you a rainbow as a sign, but His covenant with you is sure. Why not look to Him today for His answers—both for the innovative ideas you need and for the precise timing in which to do them.

We too often love
things and use
people, when
we should be
using things
and loving people.

■ ■ ■

*Be devoted to one another in brotherly
love. Honor one another above yourselves.*

Romans 12:10 NIV

16

A fable is told of a young orphan boy who had no family and no one to love him. Feeling sad and lonely, he was walking through a meadow one day when he saw a small butterfly caught in a thorn bush. The more the butterfly struggled to free itself, the deeper the thorns cut into its fragile body. The boy carefully released the butterfly, but instead of flying away, the butterfly transformed before his eyes into an angel.

The boy rubbed his eyes in disbelief as the angel said, "For your wonderful kindness, I will do whatever you would like." The little boy thought for a moment and then said, "I want to be happy!" The angel replied, "Very well," and then leaned toward him, whispered in his ear, and vanished.

As the little boy grew up, there was no one in the land as happy as he. When people asked him to tell his secret of happiness, he would only smile and say, "I listened to an angel when I was a little boy."

On his deathbed, his neighbors rallied around him and asked him to divulge the secret of his happiness before he died. The old man finally told them: "The angel told me that everyone, no matter how secure they seemed, no matter how old or young, how rich or poor, had need of me."

Honor is better than honors.

...for them that honour me I will honour.

1 Samuel 2:30

*T*he moment was a tense one. Rosalie Elliott had made it to the fourth round of a national spelling contest in Washington. The 11-year-old from South Carolina had been asked to spell the word *avowal*. In her soft southern accent she spelled the word, but the judges were not able to determine if she had used an *a* or an *e* as the next to the last letter. They debated among themselves for several minutes as they listened to tape recording playbacks. The crucial letter, however, was too accent-blurred to decipher. Finally, the chief judge put the question to the only person who knew the answer.

"Was the letter an *a* or was it an *e*?" he asked Rosalie. By this time, being surrounded by whispering young spellers, Rosalie knew the correct spelling of the word. Still, without hesitation, she replied that she had misspelled the word and she walked from the stage.

The entire audience stood and applauded, including some fifty newspaper reporters. The moment was a heartwarming and proud one for her parents. Even in defeat, she was a victor. Indeed, more has been written about Rosalie Elliott over the years than about the "unknown" winner of the event!

Being a person of truth, even when it is against us, will bring great honor.

19

It is not what a man
does that determines
whether his work is
sacred or secular,
it is why he does it.

*Whatever you do, work at it with all your
heart, as working for the Lord, not for
men...It is the Lord Christ you are serving.*

Colossians 3:23,24 NIV

After twenty years of selling cars, Bob Kamm launched a new mission for his life: to bring ethics into the car business. He joined the Nickelsen Group, a leading automotive consulting firm, and immediately helped develop the Leadership Inventory and Transformation Retreat. The five-day event costs $1,595 and is considered an intellectual, physical, and spiritual program. Says Kamm, "It's a very profound process that leads people to question who they are in this life and what they're going to do with the rest of it."

Car dealers who have come to the retreat center rarely leave the same as they come. Kamm says, "For car people it's the fourth gear at 6,000 rpm's. We're trying to get it into fifth gear at 2,300 rpm's." A slower speed is actually taught as one that helps managers become more efficient, responsive, and more in control of decisions that impact all areas of their lives.

Each participant leaves the retreat with an action plan that often involves restructuring their routines, altering their management style, and apologizing to employees. Can such change occur in only five days? Kamm believes it can...because the real motivation to work is not tasks, it's a person's inner character. Change that, and you change everything.

Character is what you are in the dark.

The integrity of the upright shall guide them.

Proverbs 11:3

$\mathcal{M}$any years ago, a boy was born in Russia who thought himself to be so ugly, he was certain there would be no happiness for him in life. He bemoaned the fact that he had a wide nose, thick lips, small gray eyes, and big hands and feet. He was so distraught about his ugliness, he asked God to work a miracle and turn him into a handsome man. He vowed that if God would do this, he would give Him all he possessed, as well as all he might possess in the future.

That Russian boy was Count Tolstoy, one of the world's foremost authors in the twentieth century, perhaps best known for his epic *War and Peace*. In one of his books, Tolstoy admits that through the years he discovered that the beauty of physical appearance he had once sought was not the only beauty in life. Indeed, it was not the best beauty. Instead, Tolstoy came to regard *the beauty of a strong character* as having the greatest good in God's sight.

So many people spend enormous sums today on their physical appearance. Character, in contrast, is not a matter of money or of looks. It is a matter of doing what is right apart from money, and of standing up for what is right apart from appearances.

The ultimate measure
of a man is not where
he stands in moments
of comfort and
convenience, but
where he stands at
times of challenge
and controversy.

■   ■   ■

If thou faint in the day of adversity,
thy strength is small.

Proverbs 24:10

*S*ome thought Les Goldberg was crazy when he cashed in his personal investments to buy a home to lease to the homeless. Goldberg, a retired engineer, felt it was the only decision he could make.

Since he retired, Goldberg has been a busy volunteer, serving on six service boards and leading a crew of homeless people at odd jobs and charity work. He spends at least an hour a day with his homeless friends and has helped renovate several properties on their behalf. In all his efforts, Goldberg never regarded the homeless as irresponsible or unreliable. He only saw them as people. He figured the house he purchased could be used as both a temporary shelter and a drop-in center...a place where homeless people might pick up mail, make phone calls, follow up job leads, and receive donated commodities. Four homeless men live at the house, paying minimal rent to offset expenses. House rules are strict—no alcohol, no drugs, no loitering.

Goldberg has never been rich. For twenty years he ran his own business, making about $25,000 a year designing and installing fire sprinklers. He simply was a man who saw a need and found a way to help meet it.

If you tell the truth, you don't have to remember anything.

• • •

A truthful witness gives honest testimony,
but a false witness tells lies.

Proverbs 12:17 NIV

*F*our young men once competed vigorously to become head of the trust department at their bank. After considering the merits of each applicant, the board of directors made its decision. They decided to notify the young man of his promotion, including a substantial raise in salary, at a meeting scheduled after lunch.

During the noon hour, the young man they had selected went to the cafeteria for lunch. One of the directors was behind him in the line, separated by several other customers. The director saw the young man select his food, including a small piece of butter. As soon as he flipped the butter onto his plate, he immediately shuffled some food on top of it to hide it from the cashier. Thus, he avoided paying for it.

That afternoon the directors met to notify the young man, but prior to bringing him into the room, the incident was told to the entire board. Rather than give the young man the promotion, they called him in to discharge him from the bank. They had concluded that if he was willing to lie to a cashier about what was on his plate, he would be just as willing to lie about what was in the bank's accounts.

Lying isn't a matter of degree. A lie is a lie. Truth is the truth. And you can bank on that fact!

Trust in yourself and you are doomed to disappointment... trust in money and you may have it taken from you...But trust in God, and you are never to be confounded in time or eternity.

■ ■ ■

It is better to take refuge in the Lord than to trust in man.

Psalm 118:8 NIV

$\mathcal{E}$arl Weaver, former manager of the Baltimore Orioles, had a rule that no one could steal a base unless he gave the steal sign. This ruling upset Reggie Jackson, who felt he knew the pitchers and catchers well enough to judge when he could steal. One day he decided to steal without a sign. He got a good jump off the pitcher and easily beat the throw to second base. As he shook the dirt from his uniform, he smiled with delight, feeling he had vindicated his judgment.

Weaver later took Jackson aside and explained why he hadn't given the steal sign. The next batter was Lee May, a major power hitter. Because first base was open, the opposing team intentionally walked May. The batter after May hadn't been strong against this pitcher, so Weaver had to send in a designated hitter. That left their team without the bench strength they might have needed later in the game.

Jackson had seen a stolen base as involving only the relationship between pitcher and catcher. Weaver was calling signals with the entire game in mind.

Don't put your trust in what you see around you. Trust the One Who sees the "big picture" that spans all of time and eternity.

The superior man...stands erect by bending above the fallen. He rises by lifting others.

∎ ∎ ∎

And we urge you, brethren, admonish the unruly, encourage the fainthearted, help the weak, be patient with all men.

1 Thessalonians 5:14 NASB

30

When British prime minister William E. Gladstone was facing one of the greatest crises of his political life, he sat down one morning at two o'clock to write a speech he hoped would help him win a great political victory in Parliament the following day.

At that hour, the mother of a poor, dying cripple saw the light on in his home and knocked at his door. She asked him to come and bring a message of hope and cheer to her son.

Without hesitation, Gladstone left his half-finished speech on his desk and spent the remainder of the night with the child, leading him to Christ before he died. As morning light was breaking, he went back to his study and faced his own day with a smile of confidence, peace, and power. He said to a friend later that morning, "I am the happiest man in the world today." When asked why, he replied that the previous night he had been allowed to serve a child in the name of the Master.

Later in the day Gladstone made the greatest speech of his life in the House of Commons and carried his cause to a triumphant success. Were the two events related? Gladstone could never be convinced that they weren't.

You can't do much
about your ancestors
but you can
influence your
descendants
enormously.

*...but as for me and my house,
we will serve the Lord.*

Joshua 24:15

*B*ill Galston was at the peak of his career when he resigned as a domestic policy adviser to President Clinton to return to teaching at the University of Maryland. Galston's reason, "To strike a new balance," between work and family.

Galston had worked more than a decade on the ideas he hoped to see come to pass. At the White House, he helped in forming the National Campaign Against Teen Pregnancy, planning the National Service Program, and working on education reform and Head Start legislation. He consulted widely with administration officials, had an excellent reputation, and loved his job. He tried integrating time with his son, Ezra, into his schedule—even bringing him to his White House office in the evening—but Galston was continually hounded by the fact that he often came home too tired to spend quality time with his son. He struggled with the contradiction between his "Putting Children First" theme for welfare and his own home. What triggered his resignation? Ezra sent him a note: "Baseball's not fun when there's no one there to applaud you."

The choices you make not only impact your future, but the future of your children. Make sure you have *their* best in mind in your decisions today.

The strongest evidence of love is sacrifice.

For God so loved the world, that he gave his only begotten Son, that whosoever believeth in him should not perish, but have everlasting life.

John 3:16

A Christian worker among the underprivileged in London was a true inspiration to a man observing her. When he asked what had inspired her Christian faith, she told him her story. As a young Jew, she had fled the German Gestapo in France during World War II. She knew she was close to being caught after she found refuge in the home of a French Huguenot. A Christian widow soon arrived telling her that she must flee immediately to a new place. The Jewish girl replied, "It's no use, they will find me anyway. They are so close behind." The widow said, "Yes, they will find someone here, but go with these people to safety. I will take your identification papers."

The Jewish woman understood her plan: The Gestapo would think she was a fleeing Jew. She asked, "Why are you doing this?" and the widow responded, "It's the least I can do. Christ has already done that and more for me." Sure enough, the widow was imprisoned in the Jewish girl's place, and within six months she died in a concentration camp.

The Jewish woman may have been able to outrun the Gestapo, but she could not outrun what this woman did for her. Personal sacrifice is the most potent witness and greatest legacy a person can have.

The man who fears
no truths has
nothing to
fear from lies.

*May your love and your
truth always protect me.*

Psalm 40:11 NIV

*R*oger was a good employee—not spectacular—but reliable, punctual, even-tempered, and always willing to go the extra mile.

Brian also did good work, but he didn't mind cutting a few corners to finish a job, or taking off a few minutes early to attend to his personal needs.

When Mr. Jones, their supervisor, announced that one of the two men would be promoted, Roger counted on his record and his reputation to win him the post. Brian lobbied hard for the job in an underhanded fashion by telling several of his co-workers that Roger had stolen credit for *his* innovative cost-saving measures, had misappropriated supplies, and was known to overextend his lunch hour. He was careful, of course, to preface all of his remarks by saying, "Just between the two of us...."

When Mr. Jones announced the following week that Roger had received the promotion, he received a rousing applause from his fellow employees. No one was surprised—except Brian. After all, Roger's reputation had preceded him.

So had Brian's.

Men will spend their health getting wealth; then gladly pay all they have earned to get health back.

■ ■ ■

People who want to get rich fall into temptation and a trap and into many foolish and harmful desires that plunge men into ruin and destruction.

1 Timothy 6:9 NIV

*T*he procedure for "How To Grow And Cultivate An Ulcer"[1] has eight steps, but one should understand at the outset that ulcers are not normally found in the stomach and it takes great persistence to grow one.

1. Eat at irregular intervals and try to keep fooling your stomach. Skip breakfast. Take your lunch on the run. Instead of a meal, have a sugar-loaded drink.

2. Try to work up an emotional upset over everything. Keep worrying about anything you can.

3. Don't take vacations. If forced to take one, be sure to take work along and make daily work calls.

4. Ignore minor symptoms such as abdominal pain, nausea, or spells of dizziness. Be tough.

5. Stick to your opinion and never accept the possibility you might be wrong. Never compromise. Keep a rigid point of view at all times.

6. Never delegate responsibility. Do everything yourself, and always attempt to do it perfectly.

7. Don't sleep more than absolutely necessary. Strive for three or four hours of sleep. Drink lots of coffee to stay awake during the day.

8. Keep going and going and going and going.

If you stay at this, you will soon have a full-blown ulcer, but you must work at it!

The first duty of love is to listen.

■ ■ ■

Wherefore, my beloved brethren,
let every man be swift to hear.

James 1:19

*I*n *Discipleship Journal*, Stephen Sorenson writes about a two-year period in which he had such severe tendonitis in both wrists that he could not even pick up his young daughter or twist open a bottle. At the same time, he was attempting to build a major addition to their home. Willy, a retired military musician came to help. Sorenson writes: "Willy came back to our house, day after day. He dug up our septic tank, cut diseased trees, and simply spent time with us. I could sense he understood my pain and our need. One afternoon as he and I walked and talked in the woods, I discovered why."

"For most of his life Willy had lived for his music, but a devastating ear problem developed, preventing him from listening to music of any kind. As a result, rather than being put off by my injury, Willy was drawn to me because of our common ground. And before we went separate ways, Willy became a Christian."

"As I look back, I don't know if I would have taken time to talk with Willy had my wrists been well. Most likely I'd have been hammering nails or running a chain saw. So 'all' I could do was listen and talk. But in God's plan that was enough."[2]

No person was ever honored for what he received. Honor has been the reward for what he gave.

The righteous giveth and spareth not.

Proverbs 21:26

As coach of the St. Anthony Friars basketball team, Bob Hurley has a stunning record—517 wins against only 60 losses, 15 state championships, five Top Ten rankings, and one national championship as of 1993. But of greater importance to Hurley are these records: nearly half of his varsity players routinely make the high school's honor roll, and all but one of his players have gone on to college, where approximately 60 percent have graduated.

Hurley has a reputation for helping his players choose a college based on academics first, athletics second. He declares players ineligible if their grades suffer: "If you're not committed to your education, how committed can you be to this team?" On the court, he is tough, impatient, noisy, and is a severe disciplinarian. On the other hand, players who honestly struggle in their studies are often treated to dinner and private tutoring sessions at Hurley's home.

Hurley has been offered numerous opportunities to leave his high school position in Jersey City, but for him, that's home. It's the place where he has invested his life. In 1992, he was honored by his city with a major banquet and rousing accolades. But the next day he was out hunting summer work for his players.

43

Responsibility is the thing people dread most of all. Yet it is the one thing in the world that develops us, gives us manhood...fiber.

■ ■ ■

Blessed is that servant, whom his lord when he cometh shall find so doing.

Luke 12:43

44

*S*ome have theorized that it is a fear of taking responsibility that led to the development of "errorless" machines—ones that allow for work to be done in a repetitive way so that it is "perfect" every time. Columbia University psychologist Herbert Terrace argues this approach. He contends that errorless machines fail to help people deal with the real world, where "you have to cope when you make a mistake."

In support of his view, he cites a study in which pigeons were taught to distinguish green from red. If they pecked a green light, they received no food. If they pecked a red light—half got food *every* time, but the other half received food on an erratic basis. When the pigeons that got a "reward" every time were switched over to the group to receive rewards irregularly, they hit their heads against the walls, flapped their wings, and started pecking wildly at everything in sight. The birds *trained* on the intermittent system didn't go wild when a correct peck failed to produce food. Instead, they stayed calm and continued pecking only at red until they were rewarded with a snack.

Responsibility is built as we take life in stride and acknowledge failures, disappointments, and faults. Own up to life today. You'll grow stronger in character.

Perhaps once in a hundred years a person may be ruined by excessive praise, but surely once every minute someone dies inside for lack of it.

■ ■ ■

Let no corrupt communication proceed out of your mouth, but that which is good to the use of edifying, that it may minister grace unto the hearers.

Ephesians 4:29

A little boy was using a super adhesive glue to put together a model airplane and he soon found his right finger bonded to a wing of the plane. The more he tried to free himself of it, the more he became frustrated. When he finally did get the wing off his finger, it brought pain that lasted several days. Needless to say, his enthusiasm for building the plane evaporated.

What many people don't realize is that their words of insult, ridicule, and criticism very often stick to others like Super Glue™. The more a person tries to free himself or herself from negative comments or a negative self-image that may have developed over the years, the more frustrated the person becomes. Failure to free oneself of the past is perceived as just one more failure! When a person's work is criticized and ridiculed, they will tend to care far less about their job. Productivity and quality may drop, and an infectious "bad morale" can set in.

What is the antidote? Praise and positive words of encouragement. People can never get too much good news about themselves. In the end, positive words strengthen people and heal them from the inside out.

Big people monopolize the listening. Small people monopolize the talking.

■ ■ ■

Seest thou a man that is hasty in his words?
there is more hope of a fool than of him.

Proverbs 29:20

A woman complained that she was coming down with the flu, so her husband took her to the doctor. Immediately, the doctor thrust a thermometer in her mouth and said, "Sit there quietly for five minutes." The woman did as she was told.

The husband was astonished and fascinated. When the doctor returned to the examining room, he pointed with enthusiasm to the thermometer and said, "Doc, how much will you take for that thing?"

Listening is truly a *fine* art, and one greatly to be cultivated as a personal trait. Those who have the ability to listen are truly valuable.

A man was considered an expert in staging sales seminars. As his new assistant was helping him set up the stage for a presentation, he gave him this advice: "One temptation I must warn you against is this: as you are conducting a meeting you will often find people disagree with some of your ideas. You may see someone shaking his head negatively as you speak. Now, the natural thing for you to do is to take out after that person and try to convince him further that you are right. Don't do it. The chances are he is the only person listening to you!"

God sends no one away except those who are full of themselves.

God resisteth the proud, and giveth grace to the humble.

1 Peter 5:5

*S*ometime, when you're feeling important!
Sometime, when your ego's in bloom;
Sometime, when you take it for granted
You're the best qualified in the room;

Sometime, when you feel that your going
Would leave an unfillable hole,
Just follow these simple instructions,
And see how it humbles your soul.

Take a bucket and fill it with water,
Put your hand in it, up to the wrist;
Pull it out, and the hole that's remaining,
Is a measure of how you'll be missed.

You may splash all you please when you enter,
You can stir up the water galore,
But stop, and you'll find in a minute
That it looks quite the same as before.

The morale in this quaint example,
Is do just the best that you can;
And be proud of yourself, but remember
There's no indispensable man.

(Anonymous)

The measure of a man is not what he does on Sunday, but rather who he is Monday through Saturday.

■ ■ ■

...that you may live a life worthy of the Lord and may please him in every way: bearing fruit in every good work.

Colossians 1:10 NIV

The story is told of two men who met on the street. One man said to the other, "Have you heard about Harry? He embezzled half a million dollars from his company." The other man said, "That's terrible. I never did trust Harry."

The first man continued, "Not only that, he left town and took Tom's wife with him." The other man said, "That's awful. Harry has always been a ne'er-do-well."

The first man said, "Not only that, he stole a car to make his getaway." The other man said, "That's scandalous; I always did think Harry had a bad streak in him."

The first man concluded, "Not only that, they think he was drunk when he pulled out of town." The other man said, "Harry's no good!" After a few moments of reflection, he then asked, "But what really bothers me is this—who's going to teach his Sunday school class this week?"

Integrity is a seven-day-a-week job. It requires an ongoing supply of character and a steady flow of trustworthiness.

The world is blessed
most by men who do
things, and not by
those who merely
talk about them.

■ ■ ■

*But be ye doers of the word, and not
hearers only, deceiving your own selves.*

James 1:22

*J*ohann Olav Koss was a star at the 1994 Winter Olympic Games at Lillehammer, Norway. A hometown favorite, he skated his way to three gold medals and three world records in the 1,500-, 5,000-, and 10,000-meter races. Perhaps no one was as surprised as Koss when he won his first medal. He said, "There was so much joy over this gold medal that it made me think a little bit before the next race...I decided, if this will happen to me again, I want to give the bonus that I get to Olympic Aid....It made me strong, I think, to be skating for someone else."

At a press conference after winning the second gold medal, Koss made his announcement: He would donate all his bonus money from equipment sponsors and the Norwegian Olympic Committee to Olympic Aid—a gift of more than $175,000. Koss challenged his countrymen to donate 10 kroner ($1.37US) for every Norwegian gold medal. The reaction caused an avalanche of funds, more than $200,000 during the games and up to a million dollars afterward.

Koss, who entered medical school after the Olympics, was surprised at all the fuss he had caused. Helping children and the less fortunate was not only his future career...it was his nature.

Authority without wisdom is like a heavy ax without an edge, fitter to bruise than polish.

■   ■   ■

...the authority the Lord gave us for building you up rather than pulling you down.

2 Corinthians 10:8 NIV

*J*ohn D. Rockefeller is known for his amazing business success, but he had a greater reputation among those who knew him as being a man who was understanding. He had a sincere appreciation for other people and was willing to accept failure if an honest attempt had been made at success.

When one of his partners, Edward T. Bedford, failed in a business venture, which cost Rockefeller's company a million dollars, Rockefeller responded with a statement that has become classic in business lore. He didn't criticize Bedford because he knew he had done his best. He did, however, call Bedford to his office and say, "I think it is honorable that you were able to salvage 60 percent of the money you invested in the South American venture. That's not bad; in fact, it's splendid. We don't always do as well as that upstairs."

There's very little to be gained by making someone feel worse regarding something they already feel bad about! Rather, the gain lies in helping someone see the beneficial side of a failure, the positive lessons that can be learned from mistakes, and to give hope for future attempts at success. Be an *encourager* to another person today. You'll both feel...and do...better!

The best way to teach character is to have it around the house.

■ ■ ■

A righteous man who walks in his integrity—How blessed are his sons after him.

Proverbs 20:7 NASB

58

$\mathcal{D}$wight Moody's father died when Dwight was only four. A month later Mrs. Moody gave birth to twins. With nine mouths to feed and no income, the widow Moody was dogged by creditors. In response to such a dire and impoverished situation, the eldest son ran away from home. Few would have criticized Mrs. Moody at that point for seeking institutional assistance or letting others help raise her children. She was determined, however, to keep her family together.

On a nightly basis, Mrs. Moody placed a light in the window, certain her son would return. Moody wrote of those days, "When the wind was very high and the house would tremble at every gust, the voice of my mother was raised in prayer." In time, her prayers were answered. Moody recalls that no one recognized his older brother when he came to the door, a great beard flowing down his chest. It was only as he began to cry that Mrs. Moody recognized her son and invited him in. He said, "No, Mother, I will not come in until I hear first that you have forgiven me." She was only too willing to forgive, of course, and threw her arms around her son in a warm embrace.

Mrs. Moody didn't change just because her circumstances did. That is the hallmark of integrity.

The man who wins
may have been
counted out
several times,
but he didn't
hear the referee.

■　■　■

Though a righteous man falls seven
times, he rises again.

Proverbs 24:16 NIV

60

$\mathcal{Y}$ears ago in a federal courtroom in New York, a sarcastic district attorney presented a jury with a glass gadget which looked something like a small electric light bulb. With a mastery of scorn and ridicule, the attorney accused the defendant of claiming that this "worthless device" might be used to transmit the human voice across the Atlantic! He alleged that gullible investors had been persuaded by preposterous claims to buy stock in the company—an obvious act of fraud. He urged the jury to give the defendant and his two partners strong prison terms. Ultimately, the two associates were convicted, but the defendant was given his freedom after he received a severe scolding from the judge.

The defendant was inventor Lee de Forest. The "worthless glass bulb" that was also on trial was the audion tube he had created—perhaps the single greatest invention in the twentieth century and the foundation for what became a multibillion-dollar electronics industry.

No matter how harsh the criticism or how stinging the sarcasm aimed at your original ideas...pursue them further. Take them to their logical end—either convincing yourself that you have erred, or using them to create something new and beneficial!

It is impossible for
that man to despair
who remembers
that his Helper
is omnipotent.

■ ■ ■

I will lift up my eyes to the mountains;
from whence shall my help come? My
help comes from the Lord, Who made
heaven and earth.

Psalm 121:1, 2 NASB

62

$\mathcal{A}$t age 33, golfer Paul Azinger was at the top of his game. He had only one problem: a nagging pain in his right shoulder, which had been operated on in 1991. After seeing the doctor, Paul received a call that changed his life. His doctor wanted him back in Los Angeles immediately for a biopsy. Paul forged a compromise: he'd do it as soon as he had played in the PGA Championship Tournament (which he won) and the Ryder's Cup Challenge. Until then, he would rely on medication and prayer. He tried to convince himself he had tendinitis, but the pain grew worse. Unknown to him, he had cancer.

Paul began chemotherapy. One morning while praying in his bedroom, he was wondering what would happen if he didn't get better. Suddenly the sun seemed to force its way through the blinds and a powerful feeling of peace swelled within him. He knew with absolute assurance that God was with him and he was in His complete and loving care, no matter what.

Two years later, Paul rejoined the pro tour, the cancer gone. He says that his main goal in life now has shifted from winning to helping people see that "God is there for them."

If there be any truer measure of a man than by what he does, it must be by what he gives.

■ ■ ■

It is more blessed to give than to receive.

Acts 20:35

*J*im Abbott conquered his disability early in life. Born without a right hand, he nevertheless became a Little League and high school baseball star, a college All-American, an Olympic hero, and a major-league standout. Perhaps his crowning moment was pitching a no-hit, no-run game in the 1993 pennant race.

His *real* fans, however, see him as far more than a pitcher. He is their hero. When Abbott heard about Erin Bower, who at age five lost a hand when a rigged tube of toothpaste exploded, he wrote a personal letter saying, "When the final out was made, a lot of things went through my mind...The only thing, Erin, that I didn't pay attention to was my handicap. You see, it had nothing to do with anything."

Disabled kids flock to the park when they know Abbott is scheduled to pitch, whether at home or on the road. He makes an effort to be with them and talk personally with as many as possible who seek him out. He spends much of his out-of-uniform time answering the 300 or more letters a week he receives from kids during the baseball season.

Abbott gives more than a fine performance with his pitching arm. He gives from his heart. In the long run, that's his main claim to fame.

Men for the sake of getting a living forget to live.

■ ■ ■

It is vain for you to rise up early, to take rest late, to eat the bread of [anxious] toil –for He gives [blessings] to His beloved in sleep.

Psalm 127:2 AMP

A young boy was walking along a road one day when he spotted a copper penny shining in the dust. He picked it up and clutched it with excitement. A penny was his, and it had cost him nothing!

From that day on, wherever he walked, he kept his head down, his eyes closely surveying the ground for more pennies—and perhaps even greater treasure. During his lifetime, he found more money to be sure. In fact, he collected 302 pennies, 24 nickels, 41 dimes, eight quarters, three half-dollar pieces, and one worn-out paper dollar...a total of $12.82. He kept his treasure safe, protecting it as a "free legacy" of wealth. He delighted in the fact that the money had cost him nothing.

Or had it? In the course of scouting out his treasure, he had missed seeing the full beauty of 35,127 sunsets, the splendor of 327 rainbows, the beauty of white clouds floating overhead in crystal blue skies, birds soaring, squirrels hopping from branch to branch in the trees above the paths on which he walked, and the brilliance of autumn leaves fluttering against a backdrop of autumn sunshine.

What he had acquired—all $12.82—certainly wasn't equal to what he had missed.

If a man cannot be a Christian in the place where he is, he cannot be a Christian anywhere.

∎ ∎ ∎

Let your light so shine before men, that they may see your good works, and glorify your Father which is in heaven.

Matthew 5:16

*M*ax had one of the worst jobs in the camp— carrying stones and planks through the mud to build a crematorium. Daily he was under the lash of the camp's infamous guard, "Bloody Krott." Yet all the while, Father Maximillian Kolbe kept smiling. One prisoner recalled, "Because they were trying to survive at any cost, all the prisoners had wildly roving eyes watching in every direction for trouble or the ready clubs. Kolbe, alone, had a calm straightforward look, the look of a thoughtful man.... In spite of his physical suffering, he was completely healthy, serene...extraordinary in character." Another said, "Those eyes of his were always strangely penetrating. The SS men couldn't stand his glance, and used to yell at him, 'Look at the ground, not at us!'"

Kolbe often let others take his food ration. He said to those who questioned this, "Every man has an aim in life. Most of you men want to return to your wives...your families. My part is to give my life for the good of all men." Kolbe encouraged others to keep hope, to lift their voices in songs of praise. One recalled, "He made us see that our souls were not dead."

Good circumstances don't make men great. Great men create good in every circumstance.

You cannot live a
perfect day without
doing something
for someone who
will never be
able to repay you.

■ ■ ■

And do not forget to do good and to share
with others, for with such sacrifices
God is pleased.

Hebrews 13:16 NIV

*B*ob Richie, a former truck driver and ex-Marine, found that the idleness of early retirement got on his nerves. So he carved out for himself an unusual full-time "volunteer job" at St. Christopher's Hospital for Children in Philadelphia. There, he makes beds, picks up toys, changes diapers...whatever needs to be done. But the activities he enjoys most are sitting for hours rocking irritable babies or walking toddlers up and down the hall all afternoon.

Richie came to his volunteer work after his own experience in a hospital. A three-packs-a-day smoker for 30 years, he'd lost a lung to cancer. He said, "My wife stayed with me the whole time. That's when I realized how important it was to have somebody there." A ward full of children fighting devastating diseases may seem like the last place that a man battling cancer would want to be. Richie sees it differently. "Being here keeps my mind off it. One reason I've done so well with the cancer is seeing how the children fight. These kids—they're the real heroes."

It doesn't take much talent, exhaustive energy, or great chunks of time to do good. But it does take a warm heart and willing hands. If you have those, you'll *find* the time, energy, and ability.

Every man is enthusiastic at times. One man has enthusiasm for thirty minutes, another has it for thirty days—but it is the man who has it for thirty years who makes a success in life.

■ ■ ■

Let us run with perseverance the race marked out for us.

Hebrews 12:1 NIV

*J*ohn Erskine was one of the most versatile and best educated men of his era—a true "Renaissance man." He was an educator, considered one of the greatest teachers that Columbia University has ever had. He was a concert pianist, author of sixty books, the head of the Julliard School of Music, and a popular and witty lecturer to a wide number of groups. He had an excitement for learning that was contagious.

Students flocked to Erskine's courses not because of his fame or his accomplished career, but because of what he believed about *them*. Erskine had a strong belief that the world did not belong to him, but to his students. He regularly told them, "The best books are yet to be written. The best paintings have not yet been painted. The best governments are yet to be formed. The best is yet to be done by you!"

It was this enthusiasm for life and his optimism for tomorrow that became his greatest attribute and legacy.

Always look forward and upward. Your greatest contributions in life—your best giving, your best caring, the best of your love—are yet to be given!

Measure wealth not by the things you have, but by the things you have for which you would not take money.

A man's life consisteth not in the abundance of the things which he possesseth.

Luke 12:15

With the national coffers depleted from costly wars, King Frederick William III of Prussia found his nation seriously short of funds as it attempted to rebuild. He refused to capitulate to his enemies, and he couldn't face disappointing his people. After considerable thought, he asked the women of Prussia to bring their gold and silver jewelry to be melted down and used as exchange for the things the nation desperately needed. As each woman brought her jewelry, she was given a "decoration" of bronze or iron as a symbol of the king's gratitude. On the decoration was inscribed, "I gave gold for iron, 1813."

The response was overwhelming. The women came to prize their gifts from the king more than their former jewels! The decorations were proof that they had sacrificed for their king. In fact, it became highly unfashionable in early nineteenth century Prussia for women to wear jewelry, but very fashionable to wear a cross of iron. It was from this that the Order of the Iron Cross was established.

The meaning of life does not lie in the possession of *things*, but rather, how we use *things* to brings true meaning to life!

The foolish man
seeks happiness in
the distance;
the wise grows it
under his feet.

■ ■ ■

I have learned, in whatsoever state
I am, therewith to be content.

Philippians 4:11

For a few long seconds, Bobby Shivar was 19 feet 9 inches away from a million dollars. Standing on the basketball court in New Orleans' Lakefront Arena, all he had to do was toss the ball through the 18-inch hoop. His wife was in the stands dreaming about a red sports car, his son was hoping for a new computer. He wanted to buy a new tractor and have enough cash for his daughter's college tuition. He bounced the ball three times, made his shot...then grimaced as the ball went left and rebounded off the rim. So much for the Gillette 3-Point Challenge promotional campaign. Bobby had won $25,000 with a whirlwind week of shooting baskets on morning TV shows, posing with tourists for photos, and signing autographs.

But then it was time to go home to tiny Beula-ville...back to fixing the aging steam pipes around Camp Lejeune...back to his neat three-bedroom brick house on a rural lot. Back to enjoying his life. "It drained me," he said. In looking back the only thing he figures he might have done would have been to practice more. But after all, it was hunting season.

We sometimes think if we could only have *more* of something, then we'd be happy. The truth is, happiness isn't a matter of more. It's a matter of choice.

Seek God first and the things you want will seek you.

But seek ye first the kingdom of God, and his righteousness; and all these things shall be added unto you.

Matthew 6:33

*J*ohn Wanamaker was an amazing man. Many people in Philadelphia know him today for the store that bears his name: Wanamakers. But John Wanamaker was also a Postmaster General for many years, and he founded a Sunday school that ultimately had four thousand "scholars" attending it. Someone once asked him, "How do you find the time to run your Sunday school in addition to your business and other obligations?" Wanamaker replied without hesitation, "Why, the Sunday school *is* my business! All the other things are just t*hings*. Forty-five years ago I decided that God's promise was sure: 'Seek ye first the kingdom of God, and his righteousness; and all these *things* shall be added unto you.'"

One of the ways a man can check his priorities is this: What things do you *not* need to put on your calendar or daily planner because they are so much a habit in your life that you would never forget doing them? Is regular church attendance that way for you? What about time spent in prayer, reading Scripture, and reflecting on God's Word? What about participation in a ministry outreach, a Bible study, or prayer group fellowship? Ask yourself today, *What habits are first in my life?*

The strength of a
man consists in
finding out the
way God is going,
and going that way.

■ ■ ■

I am the light of the world: he that
followeth me shall not walk in darkness,
but shall have the light of life.

John 8:12

*I*n *A Slow and Certain Light*,[3] Elizabeth Elliot writes: "Two young Americans with high adventure in their hearts arrived in the city of Quito, Ecuador, on their way to the 'Great Amazon Rain Forest' east of the Andes. They were going on a six-weeks trek and planned to write a book about their experiences....They had been to an army surplus store before they left home and bought everything the salesman told them they would need....What more could they want? There was, it occurred to them when they reached Quito, one thing—the language—and when they learned that a jungle missionary was in town, they came to see me....'Just give us a few phrases,' they said....They described their equipment to me with great pride, and I could see that it was not going to be of much use. I wanted to tell them that what they ought to have was a guide....

"Sometimes we come to God as the two adventurers came to me—confident and, we think, well-informed and well-equipped. But it has occurred to us that with all our accumulation of stuff something is missing....What we really ought to have is the Guide himself."

Until you make
peace with who you
are, you'll never
be content with
what you have.

*But godliness with contentment
is great gain.*

1 Timothy 6:6

*O*ne of the central characters of the "Dobie Gillis" TV show in the 1960s was Maynard, a "beatnik" with beads, sandals, and goatee who avoided work at all cost. He was more comical than intelligent. In one show, Maynard informed Dobie that he was planning to do what many rock stars were doing in that era—make a pilgrimage to the Far East to consult with a guru about the meaning of life. Maynard did his best to explain to Dobie why he felt he needed to speak with an ancient wise man and find out who he really was.

Dobie finally said to him with candor, "Maynard, you will never find yourself on a mountain in Tibet."

"Why not?" Maynard asked.

Dobie replied, "Because you didn't lose yourself on a mountain in Tibet!"

A "new us" isn't to be found on a mountain somewhere, or in any other change of physical locale. We find ourselves not by searching outside ourselves, but searching within. We must come to know ourselves—both our good qualities and our bad. Then we can seek forgiveness and change those things which are negative, and build on those things which are positive. This is how we truly find ourselves.

A gentleman is a *gentle man.*

■ ■ ■

And the servant of the Lord must not strive; but be gentle unto all men.

2 Timothy 2:24

George Washington and General Lafayette were walking together one morning when they were greeted on their path by a slave. The old man paused, tipped his hat, and said, "Good mo'nin', Gen'l Washin'ton."

Immediately George Washington removed his hat, bowed, and answered, "Good morning to you, and I hope you have a pleasant day."

General Lafayette was shocked, but when he recovered his composure he exclaimed, "Why did you bow to a slave?"

Washington smiled and replied, "I would not allow him to be a better gentleman than I."

In our days, we rarely refer to men as being gentle. But gentleness is a character trait that results from the indwelling Spirit of God in our lives! Consider this approach in thinking of yourself as a gentleman:

G — Gracious and good

E — Engaging, willing to listen

N — Nice to others, regardless of who they are

T — Taking the time to move at another's pace

L — Loving

E — Endearing by acts of kindness and goodwill

(The called man) sees himself as a steward... He's obedient rather than ambitious, committed rather than competitive. For him, nothing is more important than pleasing the one who called him.

We obey his commands and do what pleases him.

1 John 3:22 NIV

When British minister W. E. Sangster first noticed an uneasiness in his throat and a dragging in his leg, he went to his physician. It was found that he had an incurable muscle disease that would result in gradual muscular atrophy until he died. Rather than retreat in dismay, Sangster threw himself into his work in British home missions. He figured he could still write and that he would have even more time for prayer. He prayed, "Lord, let me stay in the struggle....I don't mind if I can no longer be a general." He wrote articles and books, and helped organize prayer cells throughout England. When people came to him with words of pity, he insisted, "I'm only in the kindergarten of suffering."

Over time, Sangster's legs became useless. He completely lost his voice. But at that point he could still hold a pen and write, although shakily. On Easter morning just a few weeks before he died, he wrote a letter to his daughter, saying, "It is terrible to wake up on Easter morning and have no voice to shout, 'He is risen!'—but it would be still more terrible to have a voice and not want to shout."

The person who is called is the one who hears God's call and responds with a resolute, "Yes," regardless of his circumstances.

If I take care of
my character,
my reputation
will take
care of itself.

Righteousness guards the man of integrity.

Proverbs 13:6 NIV

A number of famous quotes about character down through the years have focused on one attribute: The *hidden* nature of character:

- Character is what a man is in the dark. (Anonymous)
- The measure of a man's real character is what he would do if he knew he never would be found out. (Thomas Macaulay)
- The difference between personality and character: Personality is what you are when lots of people are around; character is what you are when everybody goes home. (Unknown)

Ultimately, *you* are the only person who truly knows the nature of your character. It's like the little boy who once came crying to his mother with the pronouncement, "Mommy, eating too many green apples can make a person sick." His mother tried to comfort him and asked, "Where did you learn this?" The little boy replied, "I have inside information."

In your private thoughts, only you know what you would do in any given situation. As *you* formulate the could's, should's, and would's of your life in accordance with God's Word, your character grows. Look within...and see what kind of man you find!

Many receive advice, only the wise profit by it.

■ ■ ■

Pride only breeds quarrels, but wisdom
is found in those who take advice.

Proverbs 13:10 NIV

*N*ext to the patient who doesn't pay his bill, the physician's most difficult patient is the one who refuses to follow "doctor's orders." A recent study revealed that up to 90 percent of all patients fail to take a complete round of antibiotics—a fact that only enables bacteria to mutate into more resistant forms. A similar percentage of patients were found to cheat on diets, continue to smoke, and fail to return for required follow-up visits to their physician...even if their lives were considered in jeopardy.

One researcher noted that teachers seemed to be among the least obedient patient groups, thinking "they can modify anything doctors tell them." Young executives also present a problem with their attitude—"Just give me enough to get by." According to one study, engineers make the best patients, since they seem to be compulsive about following explicit orders.

The net result of failing to follow a physician's prescription is nearly always *less* health in the long run, even though a condition might temporarily clear up or a disease be overcome.

That's true for the advice of most professionals...and especially so for the wisdom of God's Word.

I have never been hurt by anything I didn't say.

■ ■ ■

Don't talk so much. You keep putting your foot in your mouth. Be sensible and turn off the flow!

Proverbs 10:19 TLB

*N*ovelist John Grisham, author of the blockbuster books that become blockbuster movies, has been called "a straight arrow making his way along a very crooked path." His novels often depict sleazy lawyers, corrupt politicians, and trigger-happy officers—the underbelly of a world of wealth and respectability. His heroes, on the other hand, are generally the innocent or children, such as the 11-year-old boy in *The Client*. Grisham has said he would rather be a nice guy than resort to filling his books with sex and gore. He refuses to write anything that would offend or embarrass either his mother or his children.

Contrary to what many in the publishing world might have predicted, his approach has paid off big. Fan mail and sales from *The Firm* and *The Pelican Brief* are proof. *The Firm* now has 19 million copies in print. So far, the oldest fan to write to him was 96 years old, the youngest 10 years old. Most of his readers commend Grisham for leaving out graphic violence, obscenities, and profanities. One woman reported that his was the only novel her husband had read in 17 years.

Do you have to *be* worldly in order to win the praise and admiration of the world?

No.

Success is knowing
the difference
between cornering
people and getting
them in your corner.

■ ■ ■

Can two walk together,
except they be agreed?

Amos 3:3

94

A little boy named Jimmy was very clever for his age. What he lacked in physical stature, he made up in quick thinking.

While he was eating his lunch in the school yard one day, Jimmy was approached by three big bullies who demanded he hand over his food. Jimmy hesitated, then slowly stood up. One of the bullies came closer and said, "Are you hard of hearing? We said to hand over your lunch!"

Jimmy backed up dramatically and drew a line in the dirt with the toe of his shoe. He looked the ringleader right in the eye and said, "Now, you just step across that line."

The bully didn't hesitate for a second in responding to this challenge. He stomped defiantly across the line and demanded, "Now what are you going to do about it?"

Jimmy smiled and said, "Now you're on my side!"

His approach may not always work, but it's worth a try! Sometimes the best thing we can do in a situation is to let another person talk to the point where they think they have an ally in you because of your willingness to listen to them.

No horse gets anywhere until he is harnessed. No life ever grows great until it is focused, dedicated, disciplined.

■ ■ ■

In a race, everyone runs but only one person gets first prize....To win the contest you must deny yourselves many things that would keep you from doing your best.

1 Corinthians 9:24,25 TLB

96

*J*erry Richardson faced an important decision in 1961. As a wide receiver for the Baltimore Colts, he had a job that was considered glamorous and secure. But when he was turned down for the $250-a-year-raise he had requested, he felt the time had come to take a risk and do what he had always wanted to do: He would start his own business.

Richardson and his family moved back to South Carolina, where an old college buddy invited him to buy into a hamburger stand. Richardson took the plunge and bought Hardee's first franchise. He went from catching footballs to flipping hamburgers twelve hours a day. After hours, he scrubbed stoves and mopped floors. His reward? Only $417 a month. Some would have thought, *It's time to punt.* Tired and frustrated as he was, Richardson refused to give up. He employed the same discipline he had used on the football field to focus on making his restaurant more efficient, his employees the most friendly in town, and his prices affordable. Before long, his business boomed.

Today, Richardson heads one of the largest food-service companies in the United States, with $3.7 billion a year in sales. And he is part of an investment group that is seeking a new franchise: An NFL team!

The way to get to the top is to get off your bottom.

■ ■ ■

How long will you lie down, O sluggard?
When will you arise from your sleep?

Proverbs 6:9 NASB

With only a high school diploma, Harlow Curtice landed a bookkeeper's job with a subsidiary of General Motors. Harlow, a country boy, rose to become a company president by age 35. By the time he was 40, he had been appointed General Manager of General Motors' prized Buick Division.

Curtice made his way to the top of his profession with a flair for new ideas and action. He dared to design new styles and models. Furthermore, he personally traveled throughout the United States to inspire dealers and instill in them a renewed enthusiasm about their Buick products.

The result was that even though his career was forged in the middle of the Depression, sales of Buick cars quadrupled! His division became the second biggest money-maker in General Motors' history.

To what did Harlow Curtice attribute his success? He cited these three things: 1) He set goals for himself and required the same of the people around him, 2) He took pride in confronting and overcoming obstacles that blinded his vision, and 3) He was willing to do things losers refused to do. The result: Winning became a habit!

There are times
when silence
is golden; other
times it is just
plain yellow.

To every thing there is a season...a time
to keep silence, and a time to speak.

Ecclesiastes 3:1,7

*I*n December 1994, the *Air Force Times* reported that Army soldier Joseph Cannon, who had just ended a six-year career, had not received a single military paycheck since boot camp. Officials said that Cannon's records were lost at his first duty station and he had never complained. He missed 144 paychecks, totaling more than $103,000! It seems Cannon had lived in the barracks, eaten only in the mess halls, and when he had special needs he had borrowed a few dollars from relatives. One observer noted, "It appears he thought his room and board were the payment the military offered, so he took it all in stride and never felt deprived or overlooked. He figured somebody 'higher up' would take care of him as long as he took care of his job."

While Cannon's example may seem a major injustice or simply an example of "ignorance gone to seed," his simple trust in authority is endearing. It takes great wisdom for most of us to discern exactly when to request more and when to accept what we have in life.

*To everything there is a season....*Perhaps our prayer should be: "Tell me, Lord, what season am I in?"

Every job is a
self-portrait of the
person who does it.
Autograph your
work with
excellence.

*Daniel was preferred above
the presidents and princes, because
an excellent spirit was in him.*

Daniel 6:3

*W*hether you count cash in a bank
Or trade futures on Wall Street...
Flip burgers at a beachside stand
Or whip up pasta specials at a five-star restaurant...
Fell giant timber in the Northwest
Or split and deliver firewood...
Coach a team
Or pastor a congregation...
Publish best-selling books
Or toss newspapers in the early-morning hours...
Star on your own television show
Or repair VCRs...
Farm a large acreage
Or mow and edge neighborhood lawns...
Go out on the road as a salesman for computers
Or drive a truck loaded with machinery...
Build homes
Or clean swimming pools...
Argue cases before a judge
Or settle family disputes as a counselor...
Do your best.

There are no small jobs. Only people who perceive them as small become small in the doing of them.

The best things in life are *not* free.

■ ■ ■

Forasmuch as ye know that ye were not redeemed with corruptible things, as silver and gold....But with the precious blood of Christ, as of a lamb without blemish and without spot.

1 Peter 1:18,19

$\mathcal{D}$r. Pedro Jose Greer has become something of a legend in Miami. As an intern in 1984, Dr. Greer treated a homeless man with tuberculosis, a usually curable disease that had progressed to a fatal stage. Greer was appalled that someone in his own neighborhood could be so poor and ignorant that he failed to seek medical treatment. As the man lay dying, Greer spent four days searching the streets for the man's family, hoping the man wouldn't die alone.

Rather than merely bemoan this one case, Greer took action. He set up a clinic in a shelter—beginning with only a folding table. He took other doctors along with him. His Camillus Health Concern is now one of the largest providers of medical care for the poor in South Florida, treating 4,500 patients a year. Greer has won numerous awards for his humanitarian effort. But he has never forgotten the man who died alone. Between the three days he spends at the clinic and the time he spends in private practice, he searches Miami's worst streets looking for those who need medical care.

Greer's work costs him a lot, and yet he sees himself as blessed: "I've had the privilege of treating the sick and the honor of working with the poor."

Don't ask God for
what you think
is good; ask Him
for what He thinks
is good for you.

■ ■ ■

After this manner therefore pray ye...
Thy kingdom come. Thy will be done
in earth, as it is in heaven.

Matthew 6:9,10

A businessman was once very concerned about his ability to sell a warehouse property he owned. Since he had last surveyed the building, vandals had damaged the doors, smashed the windows, and strewn trash throughout it. The building had been empty for several months and needed other repairs due to weather and general lack of maintenance. As the man showed a prospective buyer the building, he took great pains to assure him that he would replace the broken windows, bring in a crew to correct any structural damage, mend the roof, and clean out the garbage. He felt as if he was apologizing at every turn for the condition of the building, but wanted to present the best possible face on the potential sale.

To his surprise, the buyer finally said to him, "Listen, forget about the repairs. I'm going to build something completely different on this land. I don't want the building. I want the site."

So often we attempt to present to our Creator what we think is good—justifying our actions, promising to do better, trying to put the best spin on the state of our souls. In the end, what He wants is *us*. When we give Him ourselves, He gives us the very *best* He has.

Don't be discouraged; everyone who got where he is, started where he was.

■ ■ ■

Though your beginning was insignificant,
Yet your end will increase greatly.

Job 8:7 NASB

$\mathcal{M}$ost American men hear "Montana" and think of two things, a state and a star. Joe Montana is a football great by anybody's standards. Before his retirement, he led the San Francisco 49ers to four Super Bowl victories. His stats: 16 seasons, 40,551 yards, 3,409 completed passes, 273 touchdowns, and the highest quarterback rating (92.3) of any nonactive passer in history. A town has been named after him. Fellow players and opponents alike have praised his grace and skill under pressure, and his ability to run a "two-minute drill" and turn it into a winning score.

However, early on few would have given Montana odds at making it big. He grew up in Monongahela, Pennsylvania, in the long shadows of former football greats such as Unitas, Blanda, and Namath. When he got to Notre Dame, he was seventh string. By the time he was a senior, he led his team to a 1979 Cotton Bowl comeback victory, but no NFL team seemed to want him. He got the interest of scouts only two days before the draft and was finally chosen in the third round—82nd overall selection—by San Francisco. Once there, he sat on the bench behind the starting quarterback for a season and a half!

Don't give up. There's still time on the clock!

Maturity doesn't come with age; it comes with acceptance of responsibility.

When I was a child, I spake as a child, I understood as a child, I thought as a child: but when I became a man, I put away childish things.

1 Corinthians 13:11

*O*ne of the marks of maturity is the ability of a person to accept the responsibility of their own talent—to diligently develop the inherent abilities they have been given by God and to make the most of them with joy and thanksgiving. A person who does this can become a success at any age...

Victor Hugo wrote his first tragedy at age 15.

John de Medecci was 15 when he became a cardinal!

Raphael painted his masterpieces before he died at age 37. Tennyson wrote his first volume of poetry at age 18. Pascal wrote his great works between the ages of 16 and his death at 37.

Joan of Arc did all her work and was burned at the stake at 19. Romulus founded Rome at 20. Calvin joined the Reformation at age 21 and wrote his famous *Institutes* at age 27. Alexander the Great had conquered his world by the time he was 23.

Isaac Newton was 24 when he introduced the Law of Gravity. McCormick was 23 when he invented the reaper. Charles Dickens wrote *Oliver Twist* at 25.

Age had nothing to do with the genius of these great people. They merely took full responsibility for their God-given gifts and wasted no time as they maximized every opportunity to its fullest potential.

The happiest people
don't necessarily
have the best of
everything. They
just make the best
of everything.

For I have learned, in whatsoever
state I am, therewith to be content.
I can do all things through
Christ which strengtheneth me.

Philippians 4:11,13

*M*ax Cleland was a typical All-American boy, starring in sports and voted his high school's most outstanding senior. At age 24 he volunteered for combat duty in Vietnam as a first lieutenant in the Army. One month before his return home, Cleland noticed a grenade had been accidentally dropped. Moving to retrieve it, he was thrown backward by its explosion. He looked down to find his right hand and right leg were missing, his left leg badly mangled. He tried to cry out—but shrapnel had ripped his throat.

No one expected Cleland to survive. But as he recovered from a triple amputation, he recalled two things: Paul the apostle had said that hope did not disappoint, and General George Patton had said, "Success is how high you bounce after you hit bottom."

Upon his return to civilian life, Cleland entered politics, learned to drive a special car, and traveled extensively mobilizing support for veterans' causes. At age 34, he became the youngest man ever to head the Veterans Administration, and later was elected Georgia's secretary of state. Max Cleland says, "Life doesn't revolve around an arm and a leg. People look at you the way you look at yourself."

Learn by experience —preferably other people's.

All these things happened to them as examples–as object lessons to us–to warn us against doing the same things.

1 Corinthians 10:11 TLB

*J*oseph Strauss was the engineer responsible for building the Golden Gate Bridge. He took great pride in his achievement, not only because the bridge was one of the most beautiful in the world but because it was the safest. Strauss had heard all his life that "a bridge demands its life." At that time, one death for every million dollars spent was the norm for the building of bridges. Strauss determined to beat that expectation.

Strauss took to heart the problems experienced by the Oakland Bay Bridge builders who were working at the same time. He put a doctor and nurse on the construction wharf. When his suspicions about lead poisoning were confirmed, he changed from lead to iron oxide paint on the tower splices. He insisted on safety belts, hard hats, and goggles. He even put his "bridge monkeys" on special diets in hopes of helping them counteract dizziness and vertigo. He fired men who drank on the job or who were reckless showoffs. And, he spent $82,000 on a safety net that eventually saved the lives of nineteen men.

Although unavoidable accidents did claim lives, Strauss' bridge went for 44 months in construction with no deaths—a phenomenal record—all because he rejected negative expectations and became a wise example.

It's not hard to make decisions when you know what your values are.

But Daniel purposed in his heart that he would not defile himself.

Daniel 1:8

$\mathcal{D}$uring the Revolutionary War, Anthony "Mad Anthony" Wayne became a Brigadier General at age 34. Theodore Roosevelt spoke of him as "the greatest field general America ever produced."

When the British encamped at Germantown, George Washington held a "council of war" with his advisors. Wayne was all for attacking immediately and stated his views openly from the outset. Virtually all of the other officers sat around the table to deliberate the issue, offering innumerable excuses for holding back. After all the dissenting arguments had been made, Washington turned again to Wayne, who had been sitting quietly in a corner reading a book while the other military officers debated the issue. "What would you say, General?" Washington asked. Wayne slammed the book shut, rose slowly to his feet, and with a glare at the group of distinguished officers, declared, "I'd say nothing, Sir. I'd fight."

Wayne was not a warmonger. Rather, he was a patriot. His values about the importance of individual freedoms were rock solid, and he was willing to defend his position with his life.

Know what you believe, and you very likely will know what to do.

The end must justify the means.

■ ■ ■

The just man walketh in his integrity: his children are blessed after him.

Proverbs 20:7

Thomas Barnardo is one of the great Christian heroes of the 1800s. During his work among the poor and homeless in London's East End, he built a home for destitute boys that housed 400 boys and girls. He turned The Edingurgh Castle Gin Palace and Music Hall into the Coffee Palace, a center for evangelistic and Christian activities. He built a Village for Girls that served more than 9,000 girls during his lifetime. In all, more than 60,000 children benefited from the vocational training centers and homes he built.

What is less publicized is that, in extreme cases where Barnardo found children in the hands of cruel people, he would "abduct" them—a policy which, where parents were involved, was against the law. Barnardo felt bound by a higher Law, however. He truly felt the means were justified by the end! This resolve made him vulnerable to criminal charges and to bitter custody battles, but eventually the laws were changed, not Barnardo. His successful "graduates" compelled him to continue to confront evil adults wherever necessary—graduates who were lawyers, doctors, musicians, academicians, naval commanders, businessmen, and colonial ministers of state...all of whom had once been destitute, but later rescued by Thomas Barnardo.

Adversity causes some men to break; others to break records.

■ ■ ■

If thou faint in the day of adversity,
thy strength is small.

Proverbs 24:10

A young journalist, eager to land his first job, found what seemed to be the perfect opportunity. He called the newspaper and was told that applicants were being interviewed at 10 A.M. the following day.

He worked all day to prepare both his resume and portfolio of writing samples. Upon his arrival early the next morning, to his dismay he found that nine other would-be reporters had arrived even earlier! He took his place in line and kept an anxious watch on his competitors. He recognized several of them and knew their reputation. From all outward appearances, his prospects did not look good.

Rather than give up in the face of this "adverse situation," however, he wrote a little note and handed it to the secretary, telling her it was very important her boss see it at once. When the boss read the note, he found himself eager to meet the young man who had written it. It read: "Dear Sir: I'm the young man who is tenth in line. Please don't make any decisions until you see me!"

When faced with adversity, there's nearly always a creative way through it, around it, over it, or under it. Most adverse situations are resolved. Be creative in facing your troubles today. There is a way!

A man who wants
to lead the
orchestra must
turn his back
on the crowd.

*Wherefore come out from among them,
and be ye separate, saith the Lord.*

2 Corinthians 6:17

$\mathscr{A}$ biologist once experimented with what he called "processional caterpillars." He lined up caterpillars on the rim of a pot that held a plant so that the lead caterpillar was head-to-tail with the last caterpillar, with no break in the parade. The tiny creatures walked around the rim of the pot for a full week before they died of exhaustion and starvation. Not once did any of the caterpillars break out of the line and venture over into the plant to eat. Food was only inches away, but the follow-the-leader instinct was even stronger than the drive to eat and survive!

When we find ourselves in a rut, we do well to ask ourselves these three questions:

1) *Is this rut of my own making?* We tend to choose a rut because it's comfortable and requires no risk. To get out of a rut, make new choices!

2) *Who am I following?* We adopt certain patterns in our lives because someone has taught them to us directly or by example. Make sure you are following good leaders; don't simply follow the crowd.

3) *Where am I going?* Ruts develop when we lose a sense of vision for our lives...when we are "just traveling" through life and not attempting to arrive at a destination. Goals take you somewhere!

Men are alike in their promises. It is only in their deeds that they differ.

Many a man claims to have unfailing love,
but a faithful man who can find?

Proverbs 20:6 NIV

*A*drian Thomas had seen enough. The third-generation owner of Thomas Drug Store in Meyersdale, Pennsylvania, came to a fateful conclusion one winter day in 1992. He realized he was tired of losing friends to cancer and heart disease. For 96 years, his family had sold tobacco products in the front of the store and health products in the back. He just could not do both anymore."

Therefore Thomas, his employees, and family members loaded up $2,000 worth of cigarettes, cigars, snuff, and pipe-tobacco products into boxes and took them to a parking lot to be burned. To get the fire going, Thomas first set a match to his state license to sell tobacco. Then he used the burning document to set aflame the pile of boxes.

As he watched the stash go up in smoke, Thomas told his family and employees that he could not put dollars and cents above the health of his patrons.

Nearly everybody proclaims with their mouths the importance of doing the right thing—even if it cost them something. Adrian Thomas is one of those who put his money where his mouth was.

Conquer yourself
rather than
the world.

*Similarly, encourage the young
men to be self-controlled.*

Titus 2:6 NIV

*I*n *Gone With the Wind*, at the funeral of Gerald O'Hara—a heavy drinker who dies in an alcohol-related accident—his prospective son-in-law gives this eulogy: "There warn't nothin' that come to him from the outside that could lick him. He warn't scared of the English government when they wanted to hang him. He just lit out and left home. And when he come to this country...he warn't scared to tackle this section when it was part wild and the Injuns had just been run out of it. He made a big plantation out of a wilderness. And when the war come on and his money begun to go, he warn't scared to be pore again. And when the Yankees came through Tara and might of burnt him out or killed him, he warn't fazed a bit and he warn't licked neither....That's why I say he had our good points...

"All you all and me, too, are like him. We got the same weakness and failin'. There ain't nothin' that walks can lick us, any more than it could lick him, not Yankees nor Carpetbaggers nor hard times nor high taxes nor even downright starvation. But that weakness that's in our hearts can lick us in the time it takes to bat your eye." The world of "self" is truly the toughest frontier!

He who has learned to obey will know how to command.

■ ■ ■

The wise in heart accept commands,
but a chattering fool comes to ruin.

Proverbs 10:8 NIV

*I*n the eleventh century, King Henry III of Bavaria became tired of his responsibilities as king, the pressures of international politics, and the mundane worldliness of court life. He made an application to Prior Richard at a local monastery to be accepted as a contemplative, to spend the rest of his life in prayer and meditation there.

Prior Richard responded, "Your Majesty, do you understand that the pledge here is one of obedience? That will be hard for you since you have been a king."

"I understand," Henry said. "The rest of my life I will be obedient to you, as Christ leads you."

Prior Richard responded, "Then I will tell you what to do. Go back to your throne and serve faithfully in the place where God has put you."

After King Henry died, this statement was written in his honor: "The king learned to rule by being obedient."

Each of us ultimately obeys either the righteous commandments of our Heavenly Father, or the "rule of lawlessness." We must willingly choose to put ourselves under authority, including the authority of God. To fail to do so is to have "no law" other than our own whim, an unreliable source at its best!

You must have
long-range goals
to keep you from
being frustrated
by short-range
failures.

■ ■ ■

*Let us fix our eyes on Jesus, the author
and perfecter of our faith, who for the
joy set before him endured the cross,
scorning its shame, and sat down at the
right hand of the throne of God.*

Hebrews 12:2 NIV

130

*T*homas Starzl became interested in transplants as a surgery resident in medical school. In 1958, he sewed new livers in dogs whose livers had been removed— all died within two days of the operation. A year later, he found a way to stabilize circulation and the dogs lived for a week after transplant. In March 1963, Dr. Starzl performed the first human liver transplant but his patient bled to death. That failure, and a hepatitis epidemic that spread through artificial kidney and transplant centers worldwide during the early 1960s, forced his liver program to be abandoned.

In 1968, Starzl and others reported results of new transplant trials to the American Surgical Association. All seven children involved in the study had survived transplants, although four died within six months—an encouraging but not stellar result. By 1975, only two liver programs were left in the world.

Then in May of 1981, Starzl and his team had success— 19 of 22 patients lived for long periods!

Starzl was criticized, even vilified, by the medical establishment for attempting liver transplantation...but he persevered. Today, liver transplants are routinely performed in hospitals around the world.

Let failures teach you...not trip you!

The future belongs to those who believe in the beauty of their dreams.

■ ■ ■

Anything is possible if you have faith.

Mark 9:23 TLB

132

*B*y the time she was only 16, Romana was deserted by her husband and left alone to raise her two children. Living in Mexico, she was poverty-stricken, untrained, and unable to speak English, but she had a dream for a better life. With only a few dollars to fuel that dream, she headed for Los Angeles, where she used her last seven dollars to take a taxi to the home of a distant relative.

Romana refused to live on the charity of others. She immediately found a job washing dishes, followed by a job making tortillas from midnight to 6 A.M. From her two jobs she was able to save $500, which she used to invest in her own tortilla machine. Over time, and with a great deal of hard work, Romana became the manager of the largest Mexican wholesale food business in the world. And to add to this success, Romana Banuelos was handpicked by Dwight D. Eisenhower to become the 37th United States Treasurer. She exemplified what Eisenhower had to say about dreams propelling our future: "We succeed only as we identify in life, or in war, or in anything else, a single overriding objective, and make all other considerations bend to that one objective."

The future belongs to those who see possibilities before they become obvious.

■ ■ ■

For the vision is yet for an appointed time...
it will surely come, it will not tarry.

Habakkuk 2:3

$\mathscr{R}$obert Chesebrough had a product in which he believed wholeheartedly. In fact, it was his own invention. Chesebrough had transformed the ooze that forms on shafts of oil rigs—rod wax—into a petroleum jelly that he personally found to have great healing properties. He believed so much in the healing aspects of his creation that he became his own "experimental subject." To demonstrate the benefits of his product for others, Chesebrough burned himself with acid and flame...and cut and scratched himself so often and so deeply...that he bore scars of his tests for his entire life.

Nevertheless, Chesebrough proved his point and people were convinced. They only had to look at Chesebrough's wounds and how they healed to see the value of his product...which still is an international bestseller. We know it as Vaseline.

What do you see as a possibility today? Do you believe enough in its potential to help others that you are willing to invest your time, energy, resources, and hope into developing it?

Perseverance is a great element of success; if you only knock long enough and loud enough at the gate you are sure to wake up somebody.

Ask, and it shall be given you;
seek, and ye shall find; knock,
and it shall be opened unto you.

Luke 11:9

*S*ir Winston Churchill took three years getting through the eighth grade because he had trouble learning English. It is somewhat ironic, that years later Oxford University asked him to address its commencement exercises! He arrived for the event with his usual props—a cigar, a cane, and a top hat. As he approached the podium, the crowd rose in appreciative applause.

With great dignity, Churchill settled the crowd as he stood confidently before his admirers.

He then removed the cigar and carefully placed his top hat on the lectern. Looking directly at the eager audience and with authority ringing in his voice, he cried, "Never give up!" Several seconds passed. He rose to his toes and shouted again, "Never give up!"

His words thundered across the audience. There was profound silence as Churchill then reached for his hat and cigar, steadied himself with his cane, and left the platform. His address was finished.

Churchill's six-word commencement address was no doubt the shortest and most eloquent address ever given at Oxford. But his message was also one every person present remembered all the days of their lives.

The most valuable
of talents is that of
never using two
words when
one will do.

■ ■ ■

In the multitude of words there
wanteth not sin: but he that
refraineth his lips is wise.

Proverbs 10:19

A newspaperman once visited the Jack London Historic Monument. He read a sample of London's prose and was so taken with it that he wrote it down. Later, he visited the Raiders' football camp and had a chance to read the passage to quarterback Ken Stabler.

The London quote read:

I would rather be ashes than dust!

I would rather that my spark should burn out in a brilliant blaze than it should be stifled by dry rot.

I would rather be a superb meteor, every atom of me in magnificent glow, than a sleepy and permanent planet.

The proper function of man is to live, not to exist. I shall not waste my days in trying to prolong them. I shall use my time.

The reporter then asked the quarterback, "What does that mean to you?"

Stabler answered, "Throw deep."

Getting to the heart of a matter usually requires few words, but great insight.

Nothing great was ever achieved without enthusiasm.

...for the joy of the Lord is your strength.

Nehemiah 8:10

$\mathcal{H}$andel's masterpiece, *The Messiah*, has inspired millions through the centuries. Few know, however, that George Frederick Handel composed *The Messiah* in approximately three weeks. The music literally "came to him" in a flurry of notes and motifs. He composed feverishly, as if driven by the unseen Composer to put pen to paper. It is also little known that Handel composed the work while his eyesight was failing. Or that he was facing the threat of debtor's prison because of large outstanding bills. Most people find it difficult to create under stress, especially when physical or financial problems are the root of that stress. And yet...Handel did.

He credits the completion of the work to one thing: *joy*. He was quoted as saying that he felt as if his heart would burst with joy at what he was hearing in his mind and heart. It was joy that compelled him to write...forced him to create...and ultimately found expression in the "Hallelujah Chorus."

Handel lived to see his oratorio become a cherished tradition and a popular work. He was especially pleased to see it performed to raise money for benevolent causes.

When joy is present, Jesus Christ is expressed.

Carve your name on hearts and not on marble.

■ ■ ■

The only letter I need is you yourselves!
They can see that you are a letter from
Christ, written by us...not one carved on
stone, but in human hearts.

2 Corinthians 3:2,3 TLB

142

*O*seola McCarty has spent most of her life helping people look nice—taking in bundles of dirty clothes, and washing and ironing them. She quit school in the sixth grade to go to work, never married, never had children, and never learned to drive because there was no place in particular she wanted to go. Her work was her life. It was her way of being a blessing to others. Many black people in rural Mississippi didn't even have a job when Oseola began working.

For most of her 87 years, Oseola spent almost no money. She lived in her old family home, and bound her ragged old Bible with Scotch tape to keep the book of Corinthians from falling out. She saved her money, most of it coming in dollar bills and change, until she had amassed a little more than $150,000. Then she made what people in Hattiesburg are calling "The Gift." She donated her entire savings—all of the $150,000—to black college students in Mississippi. Miss McCarty said, "I know it won't be too many years before I pass on...so I planned to do this. I planned it myself." She also said, "I wanted to share my wealth with the children." Her main hope is to see a beneficiary of her gift graduate before she dies.

She truly has left a legacy written on hearts.

One-half the trouble
of this life can be
traced to saying
yes too quick,
and not saying
no soon enough.

*Seest thou a man that is hasty
in his words? there is more hope
of a fool than of him.*

Proverbs 29:20

144

When reporters bombarded Cardinal Francis Spellman with questions during a surprise interview, he finally pointed to a mounted fish on the wall behind his desk which had this label: "If I had kept my mouth shut, I wouldn't be here."

Perhaps the most potent words in any language are the simple "Yes" or "No,"...without explanation...without elaboration. Most decisions eventually come to that point.

To reach the point of answering yes or no, we do well to ask ourselves these questions:

1) *Who besides me has to have a part in this decision?* If you are either the sole decision maker or the final decision maker, you need to make a decision!

2) *What happens if I wait longer in deciding?* In most cases, things will either get better or worse for one or more people. Weigh your decision in the balances, realizing that your decision is likely to lean in favor of the heavier weight of the argument, then decide.

3) *Does the decision have a moral dimension?* If so, hold to your values and make your decision based upon them.

You can accomplish
more in one hour
with God than
one lifetime
without Him.

With God all things are possible.

Matthew 19:26

*C*laire Townsend found the weekly production meetings at the major motion picture studio where she worked to be extremely stressful. All morning, various department heads would jockey for position. The studio had just been purchased, jobs were uncertain, and team spirit had vanished. For her part, Claire began to spend more time on her spiritual life to counteract the stress. She began to pray again, discovering the power of God's love in her life. Even so, she dreaded this time of weekly battle.

Then one day during a particularly tense meeting, the thought came to her, *Pray. Pray now.* She began to imagine God's love pulsating within her, and then shooting out from her heart like a beam. She aimed her "love laser" toward the person sitting across from her. The co-worker eyed her curiously and Claire smiled back. One by one, she beamed God's love to each person around the table as she silently prayed. Within minutes, the tone of the meeting changed from confrontation to compromise. As the group relaxed, they became more creative, and Claire came to regard the meetings as an opportunity to impart God's love.

Nobody needs to know you are turning a business meeting into a prayer meeting, but God will.

Man cannot discover new oceans unless he has the courage to lose sight of the shore.

∎ ∎ ∎

Peter got out of the boat, and walked on the water and came toward Jesus.

Matthew 14:29 NASB

When Luciano Pavarotti was a boy, his grandmother often put him on her lap and said, "You're going to be great, you'll see." His grandmother, however, had dreams of Luciano becoming a banker!

Instead, Pavarotti became a school teacher. He taught elementary school for awhile, singing infrequently at special events. His father became the one who goaded him into developing his voice, chiding him for singing below his potential.

Finally, at age twenty-two, Pavarotti stopped teaching...to sell insurance. He continued to look for something stable on which he could rely financially, in case he couldn't make it in the music world. The insurance business allowed him time to take voice lessons, and the rest is history. The opera star now says, "Studying voice was the turning point of my life. It's a mistake to take the safe path in life."

He adds with a twinkle in his eye, "My teacher groomed me. But no teacher ever told me I would become famous. Just my grandmother."

It takes courage to leave a position you consider safe and launch out in a new direction. But without taking a risk, you can never realize your potential or know all God created you to be.

"The Supervisor's Prayer"

Lord, when I am wrong,
make me willing to
change; when I am right,
make me easy to live with.
So strengthen me that
the power of my example
will far exceed the
authority of my rank.

■ ■ ■

*...to offer ourselves as a model for you,
that you might follow our example.*

2 Thessalonians 3:9 NASB

*O*ne analyst has noted that business today is organized like an army. Officers of different grades and importance are leading troops on various battlefields. They are fighting various enemies and undertaking various missions. Because the employees don't wear uniforms or have stripes and bars, one must find other ways to determine a person's rank and importance.

This analyst has suggested that one way to distinguish rank in an organization is to observe what time a person arrives at work.

If the individual arrives about 10 o'clock in the morning, then you can be sure he is an executive.

If the person comes in around 9:30, you can conclude he has some authority—perhaps as a manager or department head.

If the employee comes in promptly at 9:00, then he is probably punching a time clock and is likely a clerk or someone working on the line.

But if the person shows up before 8:00 in the morning, then he or she is most likely the president of the company.

One man with courage makes a majority.

■ ■ ■

Be strong and of a good courage...
for the Lord thy God...will not fail
thee, nor forsake thee.

Deuteronomy 31:6

While he was a pastor in Indianapolis, Henry Ward Beecher preached a series of sermons about gambling and drunkenness. He soundly denounced the men of the community who profited by these sins.

The next week, Beecher was accosted on the street by a would-be assailant. Brandishing a pistol, the man demanded that Beecher make some kind of retraction about what he had said the previous Sunday.

"Take it back, right here!" he demanded with an oath, "Or I will shoot you on the spot!"

Beecher calmly replied, "Shoot away!" The man was taken back by his response. Beecher walked away at that point, saying over his shoulder as he left the scene, "I don't believe you can hit the mark as well as I did!"

Courage involves more than convictions. It involves a willingness to speak and to act in order to bring about change—in individual lives, in families, in neighborhoods, in cities, and in nations. It's not enough to "just believe" in something. You must be willing to speak out, speak up, and stand up in order truly to be a courageous person. Your voice *can* make a difference.

A man never discloses his own character so clearly as when he describes another's.

■ ■ ■

A good man out of the good treasure of the heart bringeth forth good things: and an evil man out of the evil treasure bringeth forth evil things.

Matthew 12:35

154

*T*he story is told that General Robert E. Lee was asked by Confederate President Jefferson Davis to give his opinion about a certain officer. Lee gave a glowing report.

One of the officers in attendance was greatly astonished at his words and said to Lee, "General, do you not know that the man of whom you speak so highly to the President is one of your bitterest enemies, and misses no opportunity to malign you?"

"Yes," said Lee, "but the President asked my opinion of him; he did not ask for his opinion of me."

When we speak well of our enemies, we are doing three things: First, we increase our own value. We show that we are able to rise above cheap criticism and bestow expensive "praise" on another.

Second, we diffuse our enemy's criticism of us. Any person hearing both our praise of an enemy and our enemy's disdain for us is likely to conclude that we are better than we have been described!

Third, we reveal to others that we are diligent investigators. It takes effort to find something good to say about someone who hates you; it takes very little effort or intelligence to respond with hate or hurtful ridicule.

The greatest use of life is to spend it for something that will outlast it.

■ ■ ■

But store up for yourselves treasures in heaven, where moth and rust do not destroy, and where thieves do not break in and steal.

Matthew 6:20 NIV

A very rich man once moaned to a friend, "Why is it that everybody is always criticizing me for being miserly, when everyone knows I have made provisions to leave everything I possess to charity when I die?"

The friend paused for a moment and then said, "Well, I guess it's like the pig and the cow."

"What do you mean?" the rich man asked.

The friend said, "The story goes that a pig was lamenting to a cow one day about how unpopular he was. 'People are always talking about your gentleness and your kind brown eyes,' the pig said. 'They only speak of me in degrading terms. It seems grossly unfair. Sure, you give milk and cream, but I give even more. I give bacon and ham. I give bristles. Why, they even pickle my feet! Yet nobody likes me. Why is this?'

"The cow thought for a minute and then responded, 'Well, maybe it's because I give while I'm still living.'"

Reputations and generous acts of kindness toward others receive acclaim both during and after a person's lifetime, far more than bequests. Let people see your gifts as an extension of your life, not merely as a consequence of your death.

What we do on some great occasion will probably depend on what we already are; and what we are will be the result of previous years of self-discipline.

■ ■ ■

But I keep under my body,
and bring it into subjection.

1 Corinthians 9:27

For months Eric Liddell trained with his heart set on winning the 100-meter race at the Olympics of 1924. Many sportswriters predicted he would win. At the games, however, Liddell learned that the 100-meter race was scheduled to be run on a Sunday. This posed a major problem for him, because Liddell did not believe he could honor God by running on the Lord's Day. He bowed out of the race and his fans were stunned. Some who had praised him in the past now called him a fool. He came under intense pressure to change his mind, but Liddell stood firm.

Then a runner dropped out of the 400-meter race, which was scheduled on a week day, and Liddell offered to fill the slot. This was not really "his race"—the distance was four times as long as the race for which he had trained diligently. Even so, Liddell crossed the tape as victor and set a record of 47.6 seconds in the process. He had earned an Olympic gold medal...*and* made an uncompromising stand for his faith.

Liddell went on to become a missionary in China, where he died in a war camp in 1945. He lives in history as a man known more for his inner mettle than for his gold medal.

Our deeds determine us, as much as we determine our deeds.

■ ■ ■

Even a child is known by his actions, by whether his conduct is pure and right.

Proverbs 20:11 NIV

*I*n *The Fall of Fortresses*, Elmer Bendiner tells of a miracle that happened to him and others aboard their B-17 bomber *"The Tondelayo."* During a run over Kassel, Germany, the plane was barraged by flack from Nazi antiaircraft guns. That was not particularly unusual, but on this particular flight the fuel tanks of the plane were hit. The crew was amazed that the 20-millimeter shell piercing the tank didn't cause an explosion. The following morning, the pilot, Bohn Fawkes, asked the crew chief for the shell as a souvenir of unbelievable luck.

Bohn was told that not just one shell had been found in the gas tanks, but eleven! Eleven unexploded shells? It truly seemed to be a miracle.

The shells were sent to the armorers to be defused, and there Intelligence picked them up. Later they informed the Tondelayo crew that when they opened the shells, they found no explosive charge in any of them. They were clean and harmless. One of the shells, however, was not completely empty. It contained a carefully rolled piece of paper. On it was scrawled in the Czech language: "This is all we can do for you now." The miracle had not been one of misfired shells, but of peace-loving hearts.

No matter what a man's past may have been, his future is spotless.

■ ■ ■

...forgetting those things which are behind, and reaching forth unto those things which are before.

Philippians 3:13

*H*is name conjures up memories of booming home runs, tremendous speed, and enormous natural ability. Mickey Mantle was touched by greatness as a baseball giant. And yet, just a month after receiving a liver transplant, Mantle had the graciousness to say, "You talk about your role models. This is your role model. Don't be like me." Mantle squarely faced the fact that while he was a superstar on the field, his personal life was not one to hold out to others for emulation.

Nevertheless, in the ninth inning of his life, with two outs and a full count, Mantle hit a personal home run. With humility, a sense of humor, and an absence of self-pity, he pleaded eloquently with others to take heed of his mistakes. In return, his final days were ones marked by a great outpouring of love—not only in response to the great moments he had given on the baseball fields of the nation, but in response to his honest self-appraisal that was marked by personal pain and regret.

Because of his pleas, organ donations increased all across America virtually overnight...giving countless people what Mantle himself did not enjoy: extra innings.

Everything comes to him who hustles while he waits.

■ ■ ■

We do not want you to become lazy, but to imitate those who through faith and patience inherit what has been promised.

Hebrews 6:12 NIV

This poem confirms the principle that the man who is born the luckiest is the man who doesn't believe in luck...but in work!

The Laggard's Excuse

He worked by day
And toiled by night,
He gave up play
And some delight.
Dry books he read
New things to learn
And forged ahead,
Success to earn.
He plodded on
With faith and pluck,
And when he won
Men called it luck.[4]

Luck is always waiting for something to turn up. Labor, on the other hand, with keen eyes and strong will, turns up something!

Luck lies in bed and wishes the postman would bring him news of an unexpected inheritance. Labor springs out of bed early in the morning and lays the foundation for success with competence.

Luck whines. Labor whistles.

Defeat is not the worst of failures. Not to have tried is the true failure.

■ ■ ■

Be strong and of a good courage;
be not afraid, neither be thou dismayed:
for the Lord thy God is with thee
whithersoever thou goest.

Joshua 1:9

*F*ranklin D. Roosevelt said, "It is common sense to take a method and try it. If it fails, admit it frankly. But above all, *try something.*"

In *The Pursuit of Excellence*, Ted W. Engstrom gives this advice about the importance of trying: "Starting today, you can begin to enjoy using and developing your gifts. For a start, you may want to risk something small—like a toe rather than a neck.

"For example, if you've always wanted to write, then write something, a short article, a poem, an account of your vacation. Write it as if it were going to be published; then submit it somewhere. If you're a photographer, gather your best pictures together and submit them as entries in a contest. If you think you're a fair tennis player or golfer, enter some tournaments and see how you do. You may not win the top prize, but think how much you'll learn and experience just by trying."[5]

The first step in trying may be a course you take at a local college...private lessons...or conducting your own simple experiments. Trying is perfected by practice. Keep at what it is you want to do.

The worst failure is...*the failure to try*!

I would rather fail
in the cause that
someday will
triumph than
triumph in a cause
that someday
will fail.

Now thanks be unto God, which always
causeth us to triumph in Christ.

2 Corinthians 2:14

*C*harlie Lewis moved to Michigan after losing the 1993 mayoral election in Hickory, Mississippi, by just one vote. He decided to enjoy the quiet life of a retiree, believing the election challenge he had requested from the courts was unlikely to succeed. And then came an unexpected phone call to return to Mississippi. The state's Supreme Court had thrown out three absentee ballots cast for Wayne Griffith, the residing mayor, wiping out his one-vote victory and making Lewis the winner by a two-vote margin—115 to 113.

"It's been more than two years," the 72-year-old Lewis said in response to the news. "I guess I had forgotten about it....I think that when you get to be 72 years old you learn how to digest things." Still, he was excited about the court's decision and the opportunities that awaited him.

Lewis became the first black mayor of the tiny town of 500 nestled in the red clay hills of east Mississippi. "I waited for awhile, but the law takes a long time," Lewis was quoted as saying.

Waiting may leech some of the enthusiasm out of a victory, but if the cause is a good one, waiting never destroys the joy of an eventual triumph.

The secret of success is to be like a duck— smooth and un- ruffled on top, but paddling furiously underneath.

I laboured more abundantly than they all: yet not I, but the grace of God which was with me.

1 Corinthians 15:10

*N*icolo Paganini was a well-known and gifted 19th-century violinist. His most memorable concert, however, was one marked by "furious paddling" rather than easy success. The concert was performed with a full orchestra before a packed house in Italy. Those who heard him play say that Paganini's technique was incredible, his tone fantastic. Toward the end of the concert, Paganini was astounding his rapt audience with a very difficult composition when one string on his violin suddenly snapped and hung limply from his instrument. Paganini frowned only briefly, shook his head, and continued to play, improvising beautifully.

Then to everyone's surprise, including Paganini's, a second string broke. Shortly thereafter, a third string snapped. It seemed like a slapstick comedy routine as Paganini stood before the awed crowd with strings dangling from his Stradivarius violin. Instead of leaving the stage to repair his instrument, he stood firm. He calmly completed the difficult number on the one remaining string—a performance that won applause, admiration, and enduring fame.

Your best may very well be that performed under tough and unusual circumstances!

No plan is worth the paper it is printed on unless it starts you doing something.

But be ye doers of the word, and not hearers only, deceiving your own selves.

James 1:22

*I*n May 1969, Jan Scruggs' infantry unit was attacked by the Viet Cong. Scruggs received serious shrapnel wounds and was sent home to recuperate. He felt like one of the lucky ones.

After his Army service, Scruggs earned a degree in counseling. He began to have a dream of building a memorial to his fellow soldiers, but he let the idea drop. He picked up the dream again in 1979 after he saw *The Deer Hunter*, a powerful movie about the impact of Vietnam on a group of small-town friends. This time he was determined! Although he had no organization and very little money, Scruggs used his own funds to set up the Vietnam Veterans Memorial fund as a nonprofit organization and held a press conference to announce his plans. He assembled a tremendous volunteer team of fundraisers, and in July 1980, Scruggs and his volunteers were awarded a site next to the Lincoln Memorial. They were given five years to raise the money for construction. In a fundraising blitz, Scruggs and his volunteers raised the money needed for the Vietnam Veterans Memorial...three years ahead of schedule.

The key to success is not how big your goal...but the drive you have for reaching it!

Life is a coin. You can spend it any way you wish, but you can spend it only once.

He that is greatest among you shall be your servant...and he that shall humble himself shall be exalted.

Matthew 23:11,12

*H*orace Mann is counted among America's greatest educators. A lawyer in 1837, not a teacher, he entered politics and became president of the Massachusetts State Senate. A visionary, he saw vast possibilities for developing the public education system of the nation, and he urged improvements in education wherever he had an opportunity to speak.

Mann's pleas for education resulted in Massachusetts creating a State Board of Education as an "experiment." The board's leadership position was offered to Mann. His friends, who truly believed that his political career might culminate in the presidency of the United States, urged him to decline. But Mann accepted the position. His statement to his downcast friends became a classic: "If the title is not sufficiently honorable, then it is clearly left to me to elevate it."

Not only did the position have little prestige, but the $1,500 salary was only a fraction of what Mann had earned as a lawyer. About this Mann noted, "One thing is certain— if I live and have good health, I will do more than $1,500 worth of good." And he did. From his position he gave Massachusetts a public school system that many other states adopted, to the benefit of millions of children through the years.

Only passions, great passions, can elevate the soul to great things.

...fervent in spirit; serving the Lord.

Romans 12:11

*I*n his autobiography, Bertrand Russell identified the passions which he believed had fueled his long life. He wrote: "Three passions, simple but overwhelmingly strong, have governed my life: the longing for love, the search for knowledge, and unbearable pity for the sufferings of mankind. These passions, like great winds, have blown me hither and thither, in a wayward course, over a deep ocean of anguish, reaching to the very verge of despair."

Oh, to be a person of passion—to care so deeply that you put all personal need aside in the pursuit of the goal you desire. The passionate way may not be easy or without inner pain, as Russell eloquently stated, but intense passion is rich in the intangible jewels of satisfaction, fulfillment, and deep joy.

Failures want pleasing methods, successes want pleasing results.

■ ■ ■

No discipline seems pleasant at the time, but painful. Later on, however, it produces a harvest of righteousness and peace for those who have been trained by it.

Hebrews 12:11 NIV

An insurance salesman in Nova Scotia was told by his boss that he and other agents were not assertive enough—that they were not as outgoing as they needed to be in order to score sales. Moments after he returned to his office after this pep talk, the insurance salesman glanced out his window and had an idea.

Outside his 17th-floor window he saw a scaffold with some window washers on it. He quickly wrote a note and held it up to the window for them to see. The note asked them if they'd be interested in life, accident, or disability insurance.

The men responded, jokingly, that they couldn't stop what they were doing to talk to him, but if he wanted to join them out on the scaffold, they'd be willing to listen to him while they worked. The insurance salesman took them up on their offer! Using an extra cable on the roof, he lowered himself onto their scaffold. During the course of their conversation, he sold one of the men fifty thousand dollars worth of life insurance!

Sometimes you have to go to tough places and into tough situations—the "second mile"—to succeed.

Most of the things
worth doing in
the world had
been declared
impossible before
they were done.

■ ■ ■

With God all things are possible.

Matthew 19:26

*T*wo freight trains collided one day, and a young man named George was so struck by the tragic loss of property, that he became determined to prevent another such accident. The result was that George invented the air brake.

As he set out to demonstrate the superiority of his air brake over the then-used and dangerous hand brakes, he met with strong resistance. Most railroad executives took the attitude of Commodore Vanderbilt, who said after hearing George's explanation, "Do you mean to tell me that you expect to stop a train with wind? I have no time to waste on...fools."

George Westinghouse did not give up, however, even when his invention was rejected as being an "impossible idea." Instead, he went on to invent a railroad "frog"—an invention that appealed to railroad officials. Over time, his happy customers agreed to give the air brake a try and to have it thoroughly tested in their railway operations. Taken together, Westinghouse's system of railway signaling and the air brake did more to improve the safety record of trains than virtually any other invention for decades to come.

A good reputation is more valuable than money.

■ ■ ■

A good name is rather to be chosen than great riches.

Proverbs 22:1

A young lay preacher was invited at the last minute to preach a sermon at a church in his city. On impulse he used as his text one of the Ten Commandments: "Thou shalt not steal." The next morning, he stepped on a bus and handed the driver a dollar bill. The driver handed him back his change and he moved to the rear of the bus. Glancing down to count the change before he pocketed it, the man noticed that the driver had given him a dime too much. His first thought was, *The bus company will never miss a dime.*

He quickly changed his mind, however, feeling conviction in his conscience that the dime didn't belong to him and he needed to return it to the driver. He made his way to the front and said, "You gave me too much change," and handed the man the dime.

To his surprise the driver said, "Yes, I gave you a dime too much. I did it purposely. I heard your sermon yesterday and I was watching you in my mirror as you counted your change."

The young preacher passed the test set up for him by the driver...and gave a witness to his faith in the process. May all of our deeds so match our words!

The world belongs to the man who is wise enough to change his mind in the presence of facts.

■ ■ ■

Whoever heeds correction gains understanding.

Proverbs 15:32 NIV

*I*n the late 1970s, a General Motors plant in Fremont, California, was the scene of major conflict between management and labor. Distrust ran high, and the labor contract submitted to management that year was hundreds of pages in length. GM had spent millions trying to upgrade the facility, but productivity and quality were poor. Absenteeism was so out of control that some mornings the production line couldn't even start. In the early 1980s, GM shut down the plant.

Then in the mid-1980s GM reopened the Fremont plant in a joint venture with Toyota. They started from scratch with a much simpler and shorter labor contract. The emphasis was placed on teamwork. GM promised that executive salaries would be reduced and employee input would be considered before any jobs were given to outside vendors. Workers were organized into small teams so they could spend their time rotating among tasks, rather than being locked into one repetitive task all day.

Absenteeism dropped 85 percent. Today, the plant employs some 4,300 people and pumps $800 million a year into the area economy.

Adjusting to changing times and work methods is not a sign of weakness. It's a sign of progress!

Every calling is great when greatly pursued.

■ ■ ■

*I press toward the mark for the prize of
the high calling of God in Christ Jesus.*

Philippians 3:14

A carpenter had a brother who was a famous musician. When his brother came to visit the construction company where he worked, the foreman said, "You must be very proud to have a brother who is known around the world for his music." Then, feeling that he may have slighted his worker, he clumsily added, "Of course, not everyone in the same family can enjoy an equal amount of talent."

The carpenter responded, "You're right. My brother doesn't know the first thing about building a home. It's fortunate he could afford to hire others to build a house for him." The musician brother nodded in agreement and added, "My brother and I both work with our hands. I hold a musical instrument in mine, and he holds a hammer in his."

Not everybody is called to walk the same path through life. If that were true, we'd find our walk through life very crowded indeed! Booker T. Washington wrote in *Up From Slavery*: "There is as much dignity in tilling a field as in writing a poem." Dignity resides in a man's heart and attitude, not in his job description.

Patience is bitter but its fruit is sweet.

■ ■ ■

For ye have need of patience, that, after ye have done the will of God, ye might receive the promise.

Hebrews 10:36

*I*n the days of the great western cattle ranches, a little burro would sometimes be harnessed to a wild horse. The two would then be turned loose together onto the desert range. Bucking and raging, the wild horse would drag and pull the little burro, throwing him about like a bag of feed.

In several days, however, the two would return. The little burro would be seen first, trotting back toward the ranch with the submissive steed in tow.

Somewhere out in the wild, the horse would become exhausted in trying to free itself of the burro. In that moment, the burro became the master of the two. The slow, patient, unimportant animal became the leader over the faster, more volatile, and more prized one.

Patient, committed, methodical, and hardworking people may find themselves the brunt of abuse from those who are more rambunctious in the workplace. But in the end, they tend to accomplish more, rise higher, and win greater respect from their colleagues and those who work under them.

Choose to be patient and quietly determined today, and tomorrow will reward you.

Gentlemen, try not to become men of success. Rather, become men of value.

■ ■ ■

The just man walketh in his integrity.

Proverbs 20:7

When England needed to increase its production of coal during World War II, Winston Churchill called labor leaders together to enlist their support. He asked them to picture in their minds a parade in Piccadilly Circus after the war. First, he said, would come the sailors who had kept the critical sea lanes open. Then would come the soldiers who had returned from Dunkirk after defeating Rommel in Africa. Then would come the pilots who had wiped the Luftwaffe from the skies.

Next would come a long line of sweat-stained, soot-streaked men in miner's caps. As Churchill painted the scene for the labor leaders, he envisioned someone crying out from the crowd, "'And where were you during the critical days of our struggle?' And from ten thousand throats would come the answer, 'We were deep in the earth with our faces to the coal.'"

Not every person can become number one—not every person can reside at the top of any profession, company, or institution. Not everybody can be "the star." But every person can be a hero, a person of value, a person who plays a vital role in seeing a greater good accomplished. Every person can make a significant contribution in whatever they do.

When you are laboring for others let it be with the same zeal as if it were for yourself.

■ ■ ■

Each of you should look not only to your own interests, but also to the interests of others.

Philippians 2:4 NIV

A bus driver became annoyed with what he saw. At the end of his run lay an open field which local "litterbugs" had turned into an unofficial dump. The driver had at least a seven-minute layover there several times a day. He grew tired of seeing the mess, and one day decided to get out of his bus and spend his few minutes of waiting time picking up a few of the bottles and cans.

The next day he took along a little bigger sack and some gloves, and during each layover he gathered up a little more of the trash. After a week of doing this, he was so encouraged by the change he had made in the field that he decided to spend all his free moments cleaning up the site. He worked all through the winter months, and when spring came he decided to sow some flower seeds on the land.

By the end of the summer, some of his regular riders actually began riding with him to the end of the line just to see what the driver had accomplished. He had turned a dump into a meadow...a few minutes at a time...and the entire community benefited.

Our neighborhoods are only as good as those who live within them. Make yours an even better place for you and your neighbors to call home!

Money is a *good* servant but a *bad* master.

■ ■ ■

The rich ruleth over the poor, and the borrower is servant to the lender.

Proverbs 22:7

$\mathcal{M}$oney sends many different messages:

It may say: "Hold me and I will dry up the foundations of benevolence in your soul. Grasp me tightly and I will focus your eyes to see nothing but my image, and transform your ears so that the soft metallic ring of coins will be louder than the cries of needy people. Hoard me, and I will destroy your sympathy for others and your love for God."

It may say: "Spend me for self-indulgence and I will make your soul indifferent to anything other than your own pleasure. I will become your master and you will think that I am the only mark of power and importance."

It may say: "Give me away for the benefit of others and I will return in the form of abundant spiritual renewal to you. I will bless the one who receives and the one who gives me. I will supply food for the hungry, clothes for the poor, medicine for the sick, and send the Gospel to the ends of the earth. At the same time, I will secure joy and peace for the one who spends me in this way."

A dollar speaks in different ways to different people. It's the listener who determines which message is most persuasive.

When you do the
things you have to
do when you have to
do them, the day will
come when you can do
the things you want to
do when you want
to do them.

■ ■ ■

He becometh poor that dealeth
with a slack hand: but the hand
of the diligent maketh rich.

Proverbs 10:4

*F*or 20 years he worked in the "trenches" in hospital emergency rooms, only to find himself overwhelmed with a bad case of "burnout." He describes his work this way: "It was...years of screaming, dying, drunks, drug overdoses, terminal cancer, and exhaustion." It was at that time that Lance Gentile, M.D., enrolled in the University of Southern California's film school. While continuing to save lives on hospital late shifts, he tried his hand at writing a screenplay. *State of Emergency* was turned into an HBO movie, which led to his current job on the popular TV show, ER. No, Gentile doesn't star as part of the medical staff. He specializes in "preventive medicine" as one of the medical consultants for the drama. It is his job to monitor story lines to ensure no harm is done to make-believe patients or the show's credibility. Gentile makes sure actors use correct terminology, hold instruments correctly, and have their X-rays right side up. He has also written two episodes himself.

Gentile continues to work two weekend shifts a month in Los Angeles area emergency rooms. "It keeps me current with medicine," he says. "I like working as an ER doctor much better now that I don't *have* to."

The two most important words: "Thank you." The most important word: "We." The least important word: "I."

■ ■ ■

Don't be selfish...Be humble, thinking of others as better than yourself.

Philippians 2:3 TLB

198

*O*ne of the most important things we can ever do is to be truly thankful for our friends...and say so.

Good friend of mine,
Seldom is friendship such as thine;
How very much I wish to be
As helpful as you've been to me...
Of many prayer guests, one thou art
On whom I ask God to impart
Rich blessings from His storeroom rare,
And grant to you His gracious care...
When I recall, from time to time,
How you inspired this heart of mine:
I find myself inclined to pray,
God bless my friend this very day...
So often, at the throne of Grace,
There comes a picture of your face:
And then, instinctively, I pray
That God may guide you all the way...
Some day, I hope with you to stand
Before the throne, at God's right hand:
And to say to you—at journey's end:
"Praise God you've been to me a friend—
THANK GOD FOR YOU."

—Joseph Clark[6]

I count him braver
who overcomes
his desires than
him who conquers
his enemies; for the
hardest victory is the
victory over self.

■ ■ ■

But I keep under my body;
and bring it into subjection.

1 Corinthians 9:27

*E*skimos use a grisly but effective means for killing the wolves that ravage their traps and dog teams.

First, the Eskimo coats a very sharp knife blade with animal blood and allows it to freeze. Then he adds another layer of blood, and yet another, until the blade is completely concealed by frozen blood.

Next, the hunter places the knife in the ground with the blade up. When the wolf picks up the scent of the blood with his sensitive nose, he searches out the bait and begins licking the stick of frozen blood. The more he licks the blood, the greater his desire for more. He licks until he eventually is lapping the blade itself.

So great is the wolf's desire for more blood that he doesn't notice that the razor-sharp knife has cut his own tongue, nor does he realize the blood he is licking is his own. This ravenous thirst for blood causes him to bleed to death. He eventually is found dead at the scene, a victim of his own appetite.

In like manner, our own lusts can consume us to the point where they become our demise. Consider those things you crave, and be wise.

201

Courage is resistance to fear, mastery of fear—not absence of fear.

■ ■ ■

Yea, though I walk through the valley of the shadow of death, I will fear no evil: for thou art with me; thy rod and thy staff they comfort me.

Psalm 23:4

*I*n the winter of 1995, a fishing boat began to sink in the rough, cold waters off Vancouver Island, west of British Columbia, Canada. The two men on board quickly moved to a life raft that was tied to the sinking boat by a nylon rope. Unfortunately, the rope was tied so tightly, they could not untie it.

As the fishing vessel began to list and take on more and more water, the men knew they couldn't reboard it. At the same time, neither had brought a knife onto the life raft with which to cut the raft free from the sinking ship. Both men knew that if the boat went down, it would pull the life raft under the water...and them along with it! They were in severe danger of drowning unless they could find a way to cut the rope.

The two men began chewing the rope, alternating as each man's jaw became exhausted. One man lost a tooth in the process. They worked steadily and feverishly for more than an hour, and minutes before the fishing boat sank completely, they chewed through the rope! They survived to be rescued later by another fishing vessel.

Don't let panic keep you from taking action in an adverse situation. Do what you find to do!

Let us not say, Every man is the architect of his own fortune; but let us say, Every man is the architect of his own character.

■ ■ ■

Till I die I will not remove mine integrity from me. My righteousness I hold fast, and will not let it go: my heart shall not reproach me so long as I live.

Job 27:5,6

204

$\mathcal{B}$athyspheres are amazing inventions. Operating like a miniature submarine, bathyspheres have been used to explore the ocean in places so deep the water pressure would crush a conventional submarine as easily as if it were an aluminum can. Bathyspheres compensate for the intense water pressure with plates of steel several inches thick. The steel keeps the water out, but it also makes a bathysphere very heavy and hard to maneuver. The inside is cramped, allowing for only one or two people to survey the ocean floor through a tiny plate-glass window.

What divers invariably find at every depth of the ocean are fish and other sea creatures! Some of these creatures are quite small and have fairly normal appearing skin. No heavy metal for them! They swim freely, remaining flexible and supple in the inky waters.

How is it that fish can live at these depths? They compensate for the outside pressure through equal and opposite pressure inside themselves.

Fortitude of spirit works in the same way. The more negative the circumstances around us, the greater need for us to allow God's power to work within us to exert an equal and opposite pressure!

People, places,
and things were
never meant to give
us life. God alone
is the author of
a fulfilling life.

■ ■ ■

I am come that they might have life,
and that they might have it more abundantly.

John 10:10

206

On a bleak winter morning, Jim felt overwhelmed with a sense of failure. He couldn't stop thinking, *My life is worthless. I don't fit.* He had lost his job at age 43. Alcohol had wreaked havoc on his life and although he had been without a drink for some months and was involved in Alcoholics Anonymous, he didn't see that he had any future. The image of the shotgun in the attic began to fill his thoughts. Then he roused himself and said, "I'll go see Ted."

Ted was Jim's AA sponsor, a crusty straight-talking farmer. Jim drove to Ted's house and found him sitting by his wood-burning stove. Ted seemed genuinely pleased to see Jim and began telling him how things were going on the farm—which wasn't good. They talked for nearly two hours, with Jim doing most of the listening. On the way home, Jim realized, *I've made it through the day.* Seeing Ted had saved his life. To his surprise, it was Ted who stood at an AA meeting a week later and revealed, "A week ago, my life seemed hopeless. I had lots of troubles. Then another recovering alcoholic stopped by and cheered me up and gave me a reason to keep going."

God is truly the great beneficent Author of our lives. He orders our steps to accomplish His purpose *and* to bless and keep us.

The greatest act of faith is when man decides he is not God.

■ ■ ■

Know ye that the Lord he is God:
it is he that hath made us, and not
we ourselves; we are his people,
and the sheep of his pasture.

Psalm 100:3

A story is told about actor Charlton Heston that illustrates our need to do all we can and then trust God to do what we cannot.

It seems that during the making of the great epic movie, *Ben Hur*, Heston worked long hours with the stunt trainers to learn to drive a chariot for the movie's crucial chariot race scene. He improved greatly in his mastery over the horses and rig, but finally became convinced the task was more of a challenge than he had initially anticipated. He approached the legendary director of the movie, Cecil B. De Mille about the scene.

"Mr. De Mille," he said, "I've worked very hard at mastering this rig, and I think I can drive it convincingly in the scene. But I don't think I can win the race."

The director replied, "You just drive. I'll do the rest."

God has a way of orchestrating the various races we run during the course of our lives. He trusts us to do our part in "manning the rigs." We must trust Him to determine the result of the race. As one engineer has said, "God provides the initial input. We provide the output. And God provides the *outcome*."

A true friend never gets in your way unless you happen to be going down.

A friend loves at all times,
and a brother is born for adversity.

Proverbs 17:17 NASB

A woman named Linda once was traveling from Alberta to the Yukon. The highway was rutted and rugged, but Linda naively set out on her trip in a small rundown car. The first night on the road, she found a room at a motel near a summit. When she responded to her 5 A.M. wake-up call, she saw the mountaintops were shrouded in early-morning fog. At breakfast, two truck drivers invited Linda to join them, and since the breakfast room was very small, she did.

One of the truckers asked, "Where are you headed?" When she said "Whitehorse," the other driver said, "In that little car? In this fog? No way!"

"I'm going to try," Linda said bravely. "Then we'll have to hug you," one trucker said. Linda drew back, "There's no way I'm going to let you touch me!" The truckers chuckled. "Not like that," one of them said. "We'll put one truck in front of you and the other behind you. We'll get you through the mountains."

All morning, Linda followed the two red dots which were the taillights of the truck in front of her, with the reassurance of a big escort behind her. She made the trek through the treacherous passage safely.

Friends are those who are there to "hug" and help others as they go through tough times.

Character is not made in crisis, it is only exhibited.

■ ■ ■

I have set the Lord always
before me: because he is at my
right hand, I shall not be moved.
Psalm 16:8

*I*t was an anonymous caller who informed Erik that a certain priest named Bernard was delivering sermons aimed at subverting Germany's racial policies. Eric knew little about the priest's background and could not imagine what had compelled him to take this rash course. After all, the majority of churches, both Catholic and Protestant, had either supported the policies or remained discreetly neutral. Erik attended an evening service and found the church less than a third full. During his sermon, Father Bernard proclaimed Christ's love and asked those gathered to pray for the Jews. Several left as he preached.

As Father Bernard was removing his vestments, Erik said to him, "You are gravely misinformed." The priest looked at him with tired, sensitive eyes and said simply, "I know what is happening to the Jews. And so do you, Captain." When the priest died in Dachau, Erik concluded, "I feel a bit sorry for him. He simply did not understand the need to run with the tide, to accept the inevitable."

Although Erik and Bernard are fictional characters in Gerald Green's book, *Holocaust*,[7] they make a strong point: Character does not bend to politics.

Wisdom is the quality that keeps you from getting into situations where you need it.

■ ■ ■

I would have you learn this great fact: that a life of doing right is the wisest life there is. If you live that kind of life, you'll not limp or stumble as you run.

Proverbs 4:11,12 TLB

*S*ara Orne Jewett has written a beautiful novel about Maine, *The Country of the Pointed Firs*. In it she describes the path that leads a woman writer from her home up to that of a retired sea captain named Elijah Tilley. On the way, there are a number of wooden stakes in the ground that appear to be scattered randomly on his property. Each is painted white and trimmed in yellow, just like the captain's house.

Once she arrives at the captain's abode, the writer asks Captain Tilley what the stakes mean. He tells her that when he first made the transition from sailing the seas to plowing his farm, he discovered his plow would catch on many of the large rocks just beneath the surface of the ground. Recalling how buoys in the sea always marked trouble spots for him, he set out the stakes as "land buoys" to mark the rocks. Then he could avoid plowing over them in the future.

God's commandments are like markers for us, revealing the trouble spots and snag-points of life. When we follow God's wisdom and steer clear of what is harmful for us, life is not only more enjoyable, but more productive.

God has a history of using the insignificant to accomplish the impossible.

■ ■ ■

And Jesus looking upon them saith, With men it is impossible, but not with God: for with God all things are possible.

Mark 10:27

The world's attention was turned to the Sudan early in 1995 when Jimmy Carter engaged in a peace-related mission, attempting to resolve the bloody civil war there. He emerged with the promise of a two-month cease-fire.

For too many years, the Muslim Sudanese government in the north, and the Christian and animist rebels in the south had been at war. At issue was the northern government's imposition of Islamic law throughout the nation. Their weapons ranged from deliberate starvation to bombs and bullets. In all, more than 1.3 million lives were lost.

The cease-fire agreement was forged in what had traditionally become the prime season for heavy fighting. Was it Carter's persuasive powers alone that won the agreement? Unfortunately not, said one State Department official, "The cease-fire was negotiated on behalf of the guinea worm." It appears the combatants agreed to stop fighting largely to allow medical workers to treat those suffering from a terrible parasitic disease.

Any break in such a bloody conflict is welcome...even if it takes a tiny worm to bring it about!

It's not how many
hours you put in
but how much you
put into the hours.

■ ■ ■

Whatever you do, work at it with
all your heart, as working for the Lord,
not for men.

Colossians 3:23 NIV

A time management expert once asked a seminar group to "brainstorm" a list of all the things they could do in an hour. Among the many answers written on the blackboard were these:

Walk the dog
Mow the lawn
Have a relaxed conversation with my spouse
Visit a sick or elderly friend
Take a nap
Jog through the park
Play ball with my son
Write a long-overdue letter
Pay the monthly bills
Listen to an entire CD
Clean the fish tank
Play a set of tennis

The group laughed at some of their ideas and were serious about others. At the end of a two-minute session, they had listed more than a hundred ideas. When the management expert asked them to identify the one activity that would have the greatest *long-term* impact on their lives, the group thought for awhile. By a great majority, they chose an idea that could be explained in only one word: Pray.

The trouble with most of us is that we would rather be ruined by praise than saved by criticism.

■ ■ ■

If you profit from constructive criticism
you will be elected to the wise men's
hall of fame. But to reject criticism is to
harm yourself and your own best interests.

Proverbs 15:31,32 TLB

$\mathcal{A}$ lion was stalking through a jungle looking for trouble. Seeking to pick a fight with a passing tiger, he grabbed the tiger's tail and demanded, "Who is the king of the jungle?"

The tiger answered meekly, "You are, O mighty lion."

Next, the lion grabbed a monkey, asking, "Who do you say is the king of the jungle?"

"You, O mighty lion," the monkey humbly replied.

Then the lion met an elephant and asked, "Who is the king of the jungle?"

The elephant grabbed him with his trunk, whirled him around, and threw him up against a tree, leaving him bleeding and broken. The lion got up slowly and licking his wounds, addressed the elephant:

"Just because you don't know the answer is no reason for you to get so rough."

Being in charge, and remaining so, requires more "people skills" than many people have. In the long run, it is wiser to build cooperative relationships than to attempt to rule as a dictator. Cooperation builds relationships; hard-line management destroys them. Moreover, one day you may need your employees to be strong allies!

An atheist is a man who has no invisible means of support.

■ ■ ■

The fool hath said in his heart,
There is no God.

Psalm 53:1

*O*ne Sunday a plainly dressed, scholarly-looking man went into a church in the Netherlands and took a seat near the pulpit. A few minutes later, a woman approached the pew. Seeing the stranger in it, she curtly advised him that this was "her seat" and asked him to leave. The man graciously apologized and moved to one of the pews reserved for the poor. There, he devoutly joined in the service and left afterward without further incident.

When the service was over, one of the woman's friends asked her if she knew who it was whom she had ordered out of her pew. "No," the woman replied casually, "only some stranger, I suppose."

To the woman's great dismay, her friend informed her "It was King Oscar of Sweden. He is here visiting the Queen."

People who refuse to acknowledge the existence of God simply aren't aware of Who is walking beside them day by day. We can refuse to recognize God, but that does not mean He ceases to exist or that He stops reaching out to us with His great love. Although the Lord may remain invisible to us now, He is more real than anything we can see with our physical eyes.

A half-truth is usually less than half of that.

The Lord detests lying lips, but he delights in men who are truthful.

Proverbs 12:22 NIV

A young mother went out shopping one morning only to encounter her son on the town streets. Angry that her son had skipped school, she demanded he tell her why he wasn't in class. She listened patiently to his explanation and then replied, "I'm not accusing you of telling a lie, but I have never heard of a school that gives time off for good behavior."

At the opposite end of the spectrum was the dentist who said to his patient, hypodermic needle in hand, "You might feel a little sting. On the other hand, it might feel as though you've been kicked in the mouth by a mule."

As much as we might say we always want to be told the truth, sometimes the truth hurts. But it never hurts as much as being told a lie.

Telling the truth includes being honest about ourselves—about our own nature, our sins and our faults. It means "confessing" that we aren't perfect and that we don't always do what is right before God or in relationship to others. When we lie about ourselves, we become self-deprecating, we rarely seek ways to grow and fulfill more of our potential.

Tell the truth to others...especially to yourself!

As I grow older, I pay less attention to what men say. I just watch what they do.

Show me your faith without deeds, and I will show you my faith by what I do.

James 2:18 NIV

I'd rather see a sermon than hear one any day,
I'd rather one should walk with me than merely show the way.

The eye's a better pupil and more willing than the ear;
Fine counsel is confusing, but example always clear;
And the best of all the preachers are the men who live their creeds,
For to see the good in action is what everybody needs.
I can soon learn how to do it if you'll let me see it done,
I can watch your hands in action, but your tongue too fast may run.
And the lectures you deliver may be wise and true;
But I'd rather get my lesson by observing what you do.
For I may misunderstand you and the high advice you give,
But there's no misunderstanding how you act and how you live.

—Edgar A. Guest[8]

Some people reach
the top of the
ladder of success
only to find it is
leaning against
the wrong wall.

*But seek ye first the kingdom of God,
and his righteousness; and all these
things shall be added unto you.*

Matthew 6:33

At 43, Lenny felt the time had come to give back something to his community, so he volunteered at a street-feeding program for homeless people. Soon he was counseling the families who came for food, directing them to places that provided shelter and helping several of the men find jobs. Those who ran the program told him he had a talent for working with people and encouraged him to develop it.

Lenny had been working in a semi-clerical position as an administrative aid to a corporate executive. There wasn't any higher place he could go in his field or within the company. His one regret had been that he had never gone to college. Armed with the encouraging words of his fellow volunteers, he and his wife sold their home and they went "back to school." Both eventually earned doctoral degrees and became full-time family therapists. They opened a clinic together and rebuilt their lives, this time enjoying a much greater sense of personal fulfillment.

It's never too late to start a new career. And it's never too late to make a new start in your spiritual life. Genuine success is found in establishing a relationship with your Creator, discovering who He created you to be, then developing talents and gifts He has given you!

If you were given
a nickname
descriptive of your
character, would
you be proud of it?

*A good name is rather to be
chosen than great riches.*

Proverbs 22:1

*D*uring a lawsuit, a witness was cross-examined regarding the statements he had made about the character and habits of the defendant. The counsel for the plaintiff said, "I believe you testified a little while ago that Mr. Smith, the defendant in this case, has a reputation for being very lazy and personally incompetent."

"No," protested the witness, "I did not say that, sir. What I said was that he changed jobs pretty often and that he seemed to get tired of work very quickly."

The lawyer persisted. "Has he or has he not a reputation in the community for being lazy?"

The witness replied, "Well, sir, I don't want to do the gentleman any injustice, and I don't go so far as to say he is lazy. But I do believe it's the general impression around the community that if it required any voluntary and sustained exertion on his part to digest his food, he would have died years ago from lack of nourishment."

Although we aren't necessarily wise to make decisions based upon what we think others will think of us, it's a principle of life that when we work hard, do good work, and work for the good of all, others will recognize us as men of reputable character.

Pray as if everything depended on God, and work as if everything depended upon man.

Faith without works is dead.

James 2:26

234

A little girl really seemed to believe in the power of prayer. Her parents frequently were amazed at the boldness with which their daughter prayed, and in her unswerving confidence that God had not only heard her prayers, but was in the process of answering them in the way she desired.

One day her older brother made a little trap to catch sparrows, and the girl found this very offensive. She felt sorry for the birds that might be caught, and was angry and upset that her brother would do such a thing. When he failed to respond to her arguments and pleas, she informed him and her entire family, "I'm going to pray about this."

Three nights later her face seemed almost radiant as she said her bedtime prayers, voicing with absolute faith her belief that the traps would be futile and that no birds would be harmed. After she had finished her prayer, her mother asked, "Child, how can you be so positive about this?"

The little girl smiled and said, "Because I went out three days ago and kicked the trap to pieces."

While it may be unwise to take every matter into our own hands, we are always wise to begin by putting all matters into God's hands!

The trouble with stretching the truth is that it's apt to snap back.

■ ■ ■

A false witness shall not be unpunished,
and he that speaketh lies shall not escape.

Proverbs 19:5

$\mathcal{I}$n preparation for a dinner party, a woman stopped by a small butcher shop to buy meat for the meal. She had decided to stuff and roast a chicken as the main course. When she asked the man at the meat counter for the largest chicken he had, he reached into the cold storage compartment, grabbed the last chicken he had, and placed it on the scale.

"This one weighs four pounds, ma'am," he said.

The woman thought for a moment and then said, "I'm not sure that will be enough. Don't you have a bigger one?"

The attendant put the chicken back into the compartment, pretended to search through the melting ice for another bird, and then brought out the same chicken. This time when he weighed it on the scale, he discreetly applied some finger pressure to the scale. "Ah," he said with a smile, "this one weighs six pounds."

The woman frowned, and making some mental calculations, brightened as she said, "I'm just not sure. I'll tell you what—wrap them both up for me!"

Truth is a bond, not a rubber band.

A blind man who sees is better than a seeing man who is blind.

But blessed are your eyes, for they see: and your ears, for they hear.

Matthew 13:16

A blind man was invited to attend the wedding of a friend. The couple had chosen to be married in a village church that was known for its picturesque qualities. As the couple left the chapel, the groom's mother said to him, "What a pity that you couldn't see the chapel! It really is so lovely. And such a pretty garden around it." She repeated this before mutual friends at the reception, and yet a third time after the photos came back. The blind man just shrugged his shoulders each time and tried to change the subject.

Didn't she hear the bells? the man thought to himself. For him, the bells that had rung before and after the ceremony had been magnificent. The air had been filled with their vibration and the ground had seemed to tremble at their song. He had been astonished at how many different patterns and tones were rung from the tower, and how the bells had created an atmosphere of both joy and solemnity.

The blind man finally concluded that the groom's mother hadn't even noticed the bells—the part of the ceremony that had been, for him, the most magnificent accompaniment. She, with all her senses, had experienced only part of the beauty. He, however, had experienced all that was available to him.

Men occasionally
stumble over the
truth, but most
of them pick
themselves up
and hurry off as if
nothing happened.

*The ear that heareth the reproof
of life abideth among the wise.*

Proverbs 15:31

The story is told of a man who found an eagle's egg and put it into the nest of a barnyard chicken. The eaglet hatched with the brood of chicks and grew up with them. All his life, the eagle did what the chickens did. It scratched the dirt for seeds and insects to eat. It clucked and cackled. And it flew no more than a few feet off the ground, in a chicken-like thrashing of wings and flurry of feathers.

One day the eagle saw a magnificent bird far above him in the cloudless sky. He watched as the bird soared gracefully on the powerful wind currents, gliding through the air with scarcely a beat of its powerful wings.

"What a beautiful bird," the young eagle said. "What is it called?"

The chicken next to him said, "Why, that's an eagle— the king of all birds. But don't give him any mind. You could never be like him."

So the young eagle returned to pecking the dirt for seeds, and it died thinking it was a barnyard chicken.

What you think of your own potential not only defines who you are today, but what you will be tomorrow.

The world wants your best but God wants your all.

*For whosoever will save his life shall
lose it; but whosoever shall lose his life
for my sake and the gospel's,
the same shall save it.*

Mark 8:35

*J*oseph Ton ran away from his native Romania to study theology at Oxford. As he was preparing to return to his homeland after graduation, he shared his plans with several students. They candidly pointed out to him that he would probably be arrested at the border. One asked, "If you're arrested, what hope do you have of being a preacher?" Ton asked God about this and was reminded of Matthew 10:16, "I send you as sheep in the midst of wolves." He thought, *What chance does a sheep have of surviving, let alone converting, the wolves? Yet Jesus sent them out and expected them not only to survive, but to fulfill His mission.* He returned and preached until the day he was arrested. As he was being interrogated by officials, Joseph said: "Your supreme weapon is killing, mine is dying. My sermons are all over the country on tapes now. If you kill me, then whoever listens to them will say, 'This must be true. This man sealed his words with his blood.' The tapes will speak ten times louder than before, so go on and kill me. I win the supreme victory." The officer sent him home!

When Joseph thought to save his life, he was in danger of losing his mission. When he didn't care about losing his life, he won not only life, but freedom.

Personality has the power to open doors, but character keeps them open.

The righteous shall never be removed.

Proverbs 10:30

When Brother Denys Cormier says "food," there's a big chance he will pass you a fork. He is part of the Wandering Monks of Emmaus, an ecumenical community established in the fourth century that seeks to feed the poor. In order to do that, Cormier and others founded the Wandering Monk's Guild and Bakery. The proceeds from the restaurant fund the Children's Soup Kitchen in the same city, where some 1,130 needy children receive food daily.

At the restaurant, a hearty all-you-can-eat buffet is offered, but without price. A basket is placed at the end of the food line for donations. Most days the basket is stuffed with $10 and $20 bills. People seem willing to pay far more than the average cost of a luncheon buffet because they know the money goes toward a worthy cause.

Cormier's main concern today is the 1,000 children that the soup kitchen *doesn't* reach. He says, "I'm not going to feel right until we feed them all." Although the monks in his order traditionally wander and minister to communities along the way, Cormier has found a position from which he will not be moved, and at least two doors—one to a restaurant and one to a soup kitchen—that he refuses to allow to be closed.

Only when we have knelt before God, can we stand before men.

Humble yourselves therefore under the mighty hand of God, that he may exalt you in due time.

1 Peter 5:6

*I*n 1953 a Chicago News columnist named Harris had a large and faithful readership. One of his most famous statements was one he called "A Prayer for the President." It said, in part, "O Lord...give him the courage, not of convictions, but of Your commandments." Harris seemed to be echoing the sentiments of an earlier patriot, William Penn, who said, "Right is right, even if everyone is against it, and wrong is wrong, even if everyone is for it." Clearly the commandments of God are right for every generation, regardless of public opinion. God's law—His ideal plan for mankind—is never subject to popular vote.

When we compare our lives to God's ideal, we invariably come up short. In fact, the Word of God predicts this will be the case! The guilt we feel, however, is not intended to overwhelm us or push us into despair. Rather, we are to draw closer to God, to seek His forgiveness, and to ask for His help, that we might become more like His Son, Jesus Christ. As we seek and receive God's help, we truly are transformed into people who no longer seek easy tasks or easy lives, but people who are willing to take on hard tasks, difficult challenges, and encounters with troublesome people. When we truly fear God...we will no longer fear others.

It is possible to be
too big for God
to use you but
never too small
for God to use you.

*A man's pride brings him low, but a man
of lowly spirit gains honor.*

Proverbs 29:23 NIV

*A*lthough he was raised in church, Dwight was almost totally ignorant of the Bible when he moved to Boston to make his fortune. There, he began attending a Bible-preaching church. In April of 1855, a Sunday school teacher came to the store where Dwight worked. He simply and persuasively urged him to trust in the Lord Jesus. Dwight did, and a month later he applied to the deacons of the church to become a church member. One fact was obvious to all: Dwight knew little of the Scriptures. His Sunday school teacher later wrote, "I think the committee of the church seldom met an applicant for membership who seemed more unlikely ever to become a Christian of clear and decided views of gospel truth, still less to fill any space of public or extended usefulness." Dwight was asked to undertake a year of study, which he did. At his second interview, his answers to the deacons were only slightly improved. He still was only barely literate and his spoken grammar was atrocious.

Few would have thought God could ever use a person like Dwight. But that wasn't God's opinion. He saw in Dwight L. Moody all the raw material necessary to create a major spokesman for His Word. Moody didn't need to be qualified in God's eyes, only *willing*.

A Christian must keep the faith, but not to himself.

Go ye into all the world, and preach the gospel to every creature.

Mark 16:15

*J*ohn Hull, author of *Touching the Rock*, is blind. In telling his life story, he recounts that his mother spent two years attending Melbourne High School, lodging there with Mildred Treloar. Mildred had served as a missionary in India. While John's mother lived with her, she began attending weekly Bible classes with Mildred. Over the months, her personal dedication to the Lord was renewed and deepened as the pages of the Bible came alive for her. It was this vibrant faith that she gave to her son, John.

Where did Mildred Treloar acquire *her* faith? From her father. Mr. Treloar had desired to become a minister as a young man but was rejected by his denomination. Rather than become bitter, he poured his faith into Mildred. John's mother spent many hours reading the Bible to Mr. Treloar while she lived with Mildred and vividly recalled for John his great hope of heaven. Why was Mr. Treloar considered to be unacceptable as a minister? He was blind!

John Hull credits Mr. Treloar with much of his own spiritual formation—a blind man passing on his faith to another blind man over a 60 time span!

Truly, there is an elegance to God's plan when we are faithful to reinvest our faith in others.

He who provides for this life, but takes no care for eternity, is wise for a moment, but a fool forever.

■ ■ ■

What is a man profited, if he shall gain the whole world, and lose his own soul? or what shall a man give in exchange for his soul?

Matthew 16:26

A shipwrecked sailor was found on the beach of a South Sea island. The natives there seized him, hoisted him to their shoulders, carried him to their village, and then set him on a crudely fashioned throne. It was apparent to him that he was in a coronation ceremony, but he understood little else. Over time, as he learned their language, he discovered that the natives had a custom of choosing a new man to be king each year. Once the period of kingship was over, the man was banished to a nearby island, where he starved to death.

Not particularly liking this outcome, the sailor decided to take full advantage of his position as king. Rather than sitting idle and being waited upon, he put his carpenters to work making boats, his farmers to work transplanting trees and growing crops, and his masons to work building houses on the island. When the year was over and he was exiled, the former barren island had become one of abundance.

As we live our lives here on earth, we must never lose sight of eternity, lest we find ourselves unprepared!

Courage is contagious. When a brave man takes a stand, the spines of others are stiffened.

■ ■ ■

Stand firm in the faith; be men of courage; be strong.

1 Corinthians 16:13 NIV

When Salvation Army officer Shaw looked at the three men standing before him, he was moved to compassion. A medical missionary, Shaw had just been sent to a leper colony in India. The men before him wore manacles and fetters, the metal cutting into their diseased flesh. The Captain turned to their guard and said, "Please unfasten the chains." The guard immediately replied, "It isn't safe. These men are dangerous criminals as well as lepers!"

Captain Shaw replied, "I'll be responsible. They're suffering enough." He personally took the keys, tenderly removed the bindings, and treated their bleeding, decaying ankles and wrists.

Two weeks later Shaw had his first misgiving about what he had done when he had to make an emergency overnight trip. He dreaded leaving his family alone in the colony, but his wife insisted she was not afraid—God would protect her. Shaw left as planned. The following morning his wife was startled to find the three criminals lying on their doorstep. One of them said, "We know the doctor go. We stay here all night so no harm come to you."

Courage is like love. When you give it away, you actually plant it into the person to whom you give it.

The man who sings his own praises always gets the wrong pitch.

■ ■ ■

Let another man praise thee,
and not thine own mouth;
a stranger, and not thine own lips.

Proverbs 27:2

As a rookie forward with the Detroit Pistons basketball team, Grant Hill received more votes than any other player in the NBA as the player the fans most wanted to see play in the All-Star Game. Averaging 18 points, five rebounds, and four assists a game, Hill was certainly an All-Star talent. But his fans were responding to more than the "stat" sheet. In Hill, they found a player with grace, a man who organized a summer camp for kids and called assistant coaches Sir. Hill admits of himself, "I don't carry myself like an All-Star. I carry myself as if I'm a rookie trying to make it in the NBA and be as good as I can be. Look at the way I walk. I don't strut; I don't swagger."

To most sports writers and editors, Hill is perceived as a "regular guy"—a person who is to be admired, but someone who is down-home and easy to talk to. Hill says, "I feel I'm the best player out there, and no one can stop me. I want to beat you and embarrass you bad. But I don't want people to know that. It's like a little secret I keep to myself."

Let your fans be those who sing your praises. It will be received as far more genuine by those who hear it, than if it were sung by yourself.

Motivation is when your dreams put on work clothes.

Whatever you do, work at it with all your heart, as working for the Lord, not for men.

Colossians 3:23 NIV

*H*is teachers considered him to be a lazy student. One said he was convinced he would never amount to anything. Another said, "If Rommel ever hands in a dictation without a mistake we'll hire a band and go off for a day in the country."

That was all the incentive young Rommel needed. He immediately sat up, paid attention, and turned in a dictation without one single error. He obviously could do the work if he wanted to and if there was sufficient enticement to get him to make the effort! When the promised award was not forthcoming, however, Rommel fell back into his old ways.

Later in life Rommel did find a cause he could believe in. It fired his ambition to the extent that he was filled with driving energy, rose above the ranks, and eventually gained a reputation as one of the ablest military men in the world. Marshal Rommel became known as "the Desert Fox," one of Germany's foremost heroes in World War II.

Each person is motivated differently. For most people, the deepest motivation lies in their faith. However, the outcome of motivation is universal: It sparks the actions which will change your dreams into reality.

If God be your partner, make your plans large.

■ ■ ■

I can do all things through Christ
which strengtheneth me.

Philippians 4:13

$\mathcal{D}$r. Walter Eerdman wrote a best-seller some years ago entitled *Source of Power in Famous Lives*. In it he gave biographical sketches of fifty great men and women of history—among them David Livingstone, Jenny Lind, Clara Barton, Frances Willard, Christopher Columbus, and Oliver Cromwell.

Eerdman drew this conclusion about the people he had profiled: *"In their lives, God was a reality."*

Truly great people share a common source of power—they simply apply that power in different ways. Some have greater public success and thus to a greater degree of fame and prominence than others. Many less famous people, however, have also encouraged others with stories of personal triumphs and victories. This shows that the power which comes from having a "real" relationship with God isn't limited to "stars." It is an attribute that can be acquired by anyone, regardless of their wealth or position in society.

Genuine power from God is manifest as hope in times of disaster, calm in times of crises, direction when lost, and an enduring faith. Anyone can know this power...if they will allow God to become a reality in their lives.

Whenever a man
is ready to uncover
his sins, God
is always ready
to cover them.

*He that covereth his sins shall
not prosper: but whoso confesseth
and forsaketh them shall have mercy.*

Proverbs 28:13

*P*atrick Sullivan, an Irish-American artist from Boston, moved to the village of Asolo in the Venetian Alps, where he greatly distinguished himself for his tremendous generosity. As a result, he was knighted by the King of Italy. Then Sullivan found himself in trouble. He and his friend, Count Giuseppe Samartini, were driving along a country road with the Count at the wheel, when their car struck a boy and fatally wounded him. At the time, Countess Samartini was seriously ill and Sullivan, fearful that the news of the Count's predicament might endanger her life, took the blame upon himself. A trial date was set.

Before the trial, the Countess recovered and Samartini went to the rescue of his friend. He claimed responsibility for the accident. His action resulted in two indictments—the Count indicted for the accident, and Sullivan for willful misrepresentation.

The judge rendered this decision: The Count was acquitted because the accident was unavoidable. He also set the "knight" free, declaring that his legal offense was more than compensated by his magnanimous and self-sacrificing display of friendship.

Trust God to vindicate you today.

A great man is always willing to be little.

■ ■ ■

But the greatest among you shall be your servant.

Matthew 23:11 NASB

*M*any years ago a rider on horseback came across a squad of soldiers who were trying to move a heavy piece of timber. The rider noticed that a well-dressed corporal was standing by, giving commands to "heave." The piece of timber was just a little too heavy, however, for the group of men to move.

"Why don't you help them?" the man on horseback quietly asked the important corporal.

"Me?" the corporal responded with shock in his voice. "Why, I'm a corporal, sir!"

The rider then dismounted and took his place with the soldiers. Smiling at them he said encouragingly, "Now, all together boys—heave!" The big piece of timber moved easily with the help of the additional man. The stranger then silently mounted his horse. He said to the corporal as he prepared to ride on, "The next time you have a piece of timber for your men to handle, corporal, send for the commander-in-chief." It was only then that the corporal and his men realized that the helpful stranger was none other than George Washington.

No person is too great to help others. In truth, it is only a little person who will fail to do so.

An honest man's word is as good as his bond.

*But let your "Yes" be "Yes,"
and your "No," "No."*

James 5:12 NKJV

*I*n *Up from Slavery*,[9] Booker T. Washington tells of an ex-slave from Virginia: "I found that this man had made a contract with his master, two or three years previous to the Emancipation Proclamation, to the effect that the slave was to be permitted to buy himself, by paying so much per year for his body; and while he was paying for himself, he was to be permitted to labor where and for whom he pleased.

"Finding that he could secure better wages in Ohio, he went there. When freedom came, he was still in debt to his master some three hundred dollars. Notwithstanding that the Emancipation Proclamation freed him from any obligation to his master, this black man walked the greater portion of the distance back to where his old master lived in Virginia and placed the last dollar, with interest, in his hands.

"In talking to me about this, the man told me that he knew that he did not have to pay his debt, but that he had given his word to his master, and his word he had never broken. He felt that he could not enjoy his freedom till he had fulfilled his promise."

Your word is the highest valued currency you can carry, no matter what your wallet may hold.

Find out what you love to do and you will never have to work another day in your life.

■ ■ ■

Stand at the crossroads and look;
ask for the ancient paths, ask where
the good way is, and walk in it, and
you will find rest for your souls.

Jeremiah 6:16 NIV

For astronomer Alan Hale, there's no line between vocation and avocation, between profession and passion. Astronomy is his life. "A lot of this is hobby," he has said. "I'm an amateur astronomer who also decided to make a professional career out of it."

Hale graduated from New Mexico State University with a doctorate in astronomy, but then searched unsuccessfully for a research position. He finally formed the nonprofit Southwest Institute for Space Research, which does other research and education work besides stargazing. It is looking through his high-powered telescope, however, that continues to be Hale's great love. A concrete driveway doubles as his observatory and a basketball court. Hale's approach is a simple one: "As long as the telescope is out, I might as well point it at something." One night while aiming at a cluster of stars known as M70, he saw a fuzzy blob where no fuzzy blob should have been. He checked his star charts, then sent an e-mail message to the International Astronomical Union. His find became known as the Hale-Bopp comet, a comet some say may become "the comet of the century."

Discover what it is you love to do, and then do it with your whole heart. Who knows what you may find!

Experience is not what happens to a man, it's what a man does with what happens to him.

For whatever is born of God overcomes the world; and this is the victory that has overcome the world—our faith.

1 John 5:4 NASB

*E*arl Reum has written these thought-inspiring words about experience:

"I wish you could know how it feels 'to run' with all your heart and lose—horribly!

"I wish that you could achieve some great good for mankind, but have nobody know about it except for you.

"I wish you could find something so worthwhile that you deem it worthy of investing your life within it.

"I hope you become frustrated and challenged enough to begin to push back the very barriers of your own personal limitations.

"I hope you make a stupid mistake and get caught red-handed and are big enough to say those magic words: 'I was wrong.'

"I hope you give so much of yourself that some days you wonder if it's worth all the effort.

"I wish for you a magnificent obsession that will give you reason for living and purpose and direction and life.

"I wish for you the worst kind of everything you do, because that makes you fight to achieve beyond what you normally would.

"I wish you the experience of leadership."[10]

It is the character
of very few men
to honor without
envy a friend who
has prospered.

A friend loves at all times.

Proverbs 17:17 NRSV

*L*eonard Bernstein, the famous orchestra conductor, was once asked by an admirer, "What is the hardest instrument to play?"

Bernstein responded without hesitation, "Second fiddle. I can always get plenty of first violinists, but to find one who plays second violin with as much enthusiasm or second French horn or second flute, now that's a problem. And yet if no one plays second, we have no harmony."

Leaders cannot lead without followers, contributors, supporters, those willing to help without fanfare. Without leadership, any institution or organization of any size fails to move forward. Without those who follow enthusiastically, no institution has strength. Envy, then, can kill both progress and stability!

A true friend chooses to rejoice with those who succeed rather than envy them. This can be difficult at times, but when the glow of the success or blessing grows dim, the friendship remains brighter and more satisfying than ever.

A man who does
not read good books
has no advantage
over the man
who *can't* read them.

*Apply thine heart unto instruction, and
thine ears to the words of knowledge.*

Proverbs 23:12

$\mathcal{P}$at Newbury, owner of several McDonald's franchises, was concerned that some of the adults he hired were flipping hamburgers for a living because they weren't qualified to do anything else. So he began paying his high-school-aged employees to do their homework for one hour before or after their shifts. To qualify, a student had to tell his manager he planned to study, do his homework in a designated booth, be in uniform, and not smoke. "We can't testify as to what goes into their brains," Newbury has said, "But at least we know that their books are open and they are in a position to learn."

Newbury also started a program called "Golden Achiever Points." He awards employees for good grades— 1,000 points for an A, 500 points for a B. The points are redeemable for merchandise, theater tickets, or money for college tuition and books. "It is critical that young people prepare for the work force," Newbury has said. But his programs also have made good business sense. "To attract the best employees, I need to offer benefits that are sensible to them."

Never stop valuing education. Make it a point to learn something new every day. It's your ticket to greater understanding of tomorrow's problems!

Never allow your sense of self to become associated with your sense of job. If your job vanishes, your self doesn't.

■ ■ ■

What advantage does man have in all his work which he does under the sun? A generation goes and a generation comes, but the earth remains forever.

Ecclesiastes 1:3,4 NASB

A businessman hurriedly plunked a dollar into the cup of a man who was selling flowers on a street corner and rushed away. Half a block down the street, he suddenly whirled about and made his way back to the beggar. "I'm sorry," he said, picking out a flower from the bunch that the beggar had in a canister beside him. "In my haste I failed to make my purchase. After all, you are a businessman just like me. Your merchandise is fairly priced and of good quality. I trust you won't be upset with my failure to take more care in my purchase." And with that, the businessman smiled and walked away with a flower in hand.

At lunch a few weeks later, the businessman was approached by a neatly dressed, handsome man, who introduced himself and then said, "I'm sure you don't remember me, and I don't even know your name, but your face is one I will never forget. You are the man who inspired me to make something of myself. I was a vagrant selling wilted flowers until you gave me back my self-respect. Now I believe I am a businessman."

Self-respect is vital to every person. Purpose in your heart to build up the respect and self-esteem of others. In so doing, you'll be building more respect for yourself!

Many a man has
found the acquisition
of wealth only
a change, not an
end, of miseries.

He who loves money will not be
satisfied with money, nor he who
loves abundance with its income.

Ecclesiastes 5:10 NASB

$\mathcal{H}$. Ross Perot, internationally famous billionaire, entrepreneur, and politician, was once quoted as saying, "Guys, just remember, if you get real lucky, if you make a lot of money, if you go out and buy a lot of stuff—it's gonna break. You got your biggest, fanciest mansion in the world. It has air conditioning. Its got a pool. Just think of all the pumps that are going to go out. Or go to a yacht basin any place in the world. Nobody is smiling, and I'll tell you why. Something broke that morning. The generator's out; the microwave oven doesn't work....Things just don't mean happiness."

When you look around today at the things you possess, ask yourself a question, "What is likely to be in existence 200 years from now?"

Very likely, nothing you currently own, occupy, or consider to be yours will still have any association with your family tree, and virtually everything you have may be someone's garbage one day. The "things" of life simply aren't permanent. What is lasting is the love we share and pass on to the next generation.

I am defeated, and know it, if I meet any human being from whom I find myself unable to learn anything.

■ ■ ■

A wise man will hear, and will increase learning; and a man of understanding shall attain unto wise counsels.

Proverbs 1:5

A scientist was unjustly convicted of a major crime, and found himself imprisoned with a long-term sentence in a facility located in the middle of a desert. His cell mate turned out to be a fellow scientist. Determined to escape, the first man tried to convince his cell mate to break out with him, but the man refused. Eventually after much planning, and with the help of other inmates, the scientist made his escape. But in the heat of the desert, with no food or water, and failing to locate another human being, he was forced to return to the prison. He reported his terrible experience to the other scientist, who surprised him by saying, "Yes, I know. I tried it and failed for the same reasons."

The first scientist responded bitterly, "For heaven's sake, man, why didn't you tell me what it was like out there?" The cell mate replied with a question of his own, "Who publishes negative results?"

Some people won't listen to anybody else, no matter who the person is or how experienced he or she may be. They will always have to "learn the hard way." On the other hand, a person can choose to learn from others and to glean from their experience. The first person is called a fool. The latter, brilliant.

Show me a man
who cannot bother
to do little things
and I'll show you
a man who cannot
be trusted to do
big things.

■ ■ ■

You have been faithful and
trustworthy over a little; I will put
you in charge of much.

Matthew 25:21 AMP

282

A man was walking the streets of Philadelphia searching for employment and finally happened to call on the office of a well-known businessman by the name of Girard. When he asked for a job, Mr. Girard personally responded, "Yes, I can give you work. See that pile of bricks out there? Carry them to the other end of the yard and stack them up."

By nightfall the man reported that the project was completed and he received his pay. He then asked if there would be more work the next day. Girard said, "Yes, come in tomorrow and carry those same bricks back to where you found them." The following morning the man arrived early and got busy, never saying a word. For more than a week, Girard instructed the worker to carry bricks back and forth until it was evident to Girard that he could trust this new employee. He was then given a new and bigger responsibility. As far as Girard was concerned, if the man could be faithful in a mindless, inconsequential task...he could be faithful in a transaction which truly mattered.

You have no idea who may be watching *how* you work today, even more than watching what you do. Do each task as if it truly mattered...it *does*!

The most difficult secret for a man to keep is the opinion he has of himself.

■ ■ ■

I warn every one among you...
not to have an exaggerated opinion
of his own importance; but to rate his
ability with sober judgment.

Romans 12:3 AMP

A little boy struggled to rehang the growth chart that had come off the inside of his closet door. He finally got it hung as straight as possible. Then he backed up against it, placed a ruler against his head, and reached up to mark the place on the chart where the ruler touched it. "I've grown ten inches," he cried in joy as he ran to the kitchen to tell his mother the new measurement. "I'm four feet eleven inches tall!"

His mother recognized that something must be amiss so she followed him back to his room. She quickly noted what had happened. First, the boy had hung the chart so the bottom of it touched the floor, instead of being hung six inches above the floor as called for on the chart's instructions. Then, when holding the ruler he had held it at an angle.

The boy was disappointed as his mother adjusted the chart and then remeasured him. "If you hadn't measured yourself," she asked, "would you have been happy with a growth of an inch and a half? That's really a lot for just one summer." The boy thought for a moment and then said, "Well, at least I didn't shrink."

When measuring spiritual growth we need to leave the measuring up to God, not ourselves.

No one ever said on their deathbed: I wish I would have spent more time at work!

Then I considered all that my hands had done and the toil I had spent in doing it, and again, all was vanity and a chasing after wind.

Ecclesiastes 2:11 NRSV

*O*ur grandparents may have worked hard, with less sophisticated technology, but most analysts today agree that at the day's end, our grandparents gave themselves a chance to unwind. In today's world, there seems to be no downtime. The home has become a branch of the office—with cell phones in cars, beepers in pockets, and home offices that have e-mail, fax machines, and answering machines requiring attention. Some have estimated that more than 80 percent of all white-collar employees take work home as a daily habit.

A report in *Newsweek* magazine quoted Dr. Mark Moskowitz of Boston University Medical Center as saying, "A lot of people are working 24 hours a day, seven days a week, even when they're not technically at work."[11] Moskowitz sees this as a classic formula for first-class exhaustion. Stewart Noyce would probably agree. He is reported in the same magazine issue to have slept *for an entire week* on his couch in a fit of exhaustion after graduating from business school. Noyce concluded, "It's really important to have some balance. Otherwise, it won't be fun anymore."

The writer of Ecclesiastes would no doubt say today, "There's a time for work...and for breaks!"

There is one thing alone that stands the brunt of life throughout its length: a quiet conscience.

■ ■ ■

If our hearts do not condemn us, we have confidence before God.

1 John 3:21 NIV

*A*mong the items in the Mark Twain Memorial in Hartford, Connecticut, are these words neatly framed: "Always do right. It will gratify some people and astonish the rest. Truly yours, Mark Twain. New York, February 16, 1901."

Conscience is what leads a person to do right. A conscience is created from the first lessons we learn about right and wrong. If we are never taught those lessons, we fail to develop a conscience. If we are taught them poorly or incompletely, we develop a stunted conscience. If we override our conscience and refuse to obey its inner advice, we develop a hardened conscience, and over time, we will live as if we don't have one. Without a conscience, our lives are lawless, immoral, and tainted—without character.

You can't see a conscience or autopsy it...but you can hear it whispering in your mind and feel it tugging at your heart. Nurture your conscience. Keep reinforcing what you know to be right and wrong. One way to do that is to read aloud the Word of God, or to hear the Word of God read or preached publicly.

Above all, don't take your conscience for granted. It is either healthy or becoming unhealthy...and as it goes, so goes your reputation and the quality of your life.

Shallow men believe in luck ...strong men believe in cause and effect.

Be not deceived; God is not mocked:
for whatsoever a man soweth,
that shall he also reap.

Galatians 6:7

*S*ix months after *Ebony* magazine premiered in the market, it was a runaway success with readers, but on the verge of bankruptcy for lack of advertisers. John Johnson, founder of the magazine, was encouraged by his mother to contact Zenith as an advertiser, since all of her friends owned Zenith radios. Johnson called upon Eugene McDonald, president of Zenith, who was impressed with his pluck and agreed to an appointment...but only if Johnson wouldn't talk advertising!

Johnson researched McDonald's life and learned that he was an amateur explorer who greatly admired the black explorer Matthew Henson. During the meeting Johnson discussed Henson, not Zenith radios. McDonald was so impressed with the fact that Johnson had cared enough to research his interests, he voluntarily gave the young publisher an ad, and then he called his friends at Quaker Oats, Swift, Elgin Watch and several other companies and persuaded *them* to place ads.

A lucky break for Johnson and *Ebony* magazine? Hardly. It was a good seed planted in fertile soil at the right time and in the right climate. Such seeds nearly always yield a harvest.

Dost thou love life?
Then do not
squander time,
for that is stuff life
is made of.

Remember how short my time is.

Psalm 89:47

A little boy once overheard his father saying to someone on the phone, "Yes, you may put me down for membership. I already belong to a dozen organizations, so I might as well join one more."

After his father hung up, the boy asked innocently, "Daddy, do all those groups you belong to know that you belong?"

The boy's question started the man thinking. He concluded that he was frittering away his energy trying to belong to every group that called his name. He was "belonging" to much but "accomplishing" very little. So he dropped out of most of the organizations of which he was a "member," then put his whole heart into the few he considered the most worthwhile. In these groups, he soon became an outstanding figure and a genuine contributor. Over time, he became well known in the community, not for his many memberships, but for the many good works his few memberships yielded. For his part, the man no longer had any question as to whether or not he belonged.

The man who tightly focuses his efforts is always more productive and effective than the man who allows his time and energy to be scattered among too many commitments.

A man of honor regrets a discreditable act even when it has worked.

A wise man's heart directs him toward the right, but the foolish man's heart directs him toward the left.

Ecclesiastes 10:2 NASB

The story is told of two brothers who were convicted of stealing sheep. They each were branded on the forehead with the letters ST, for "sheep thief."

One brother immediately ran away from the area and attempted to build a new life in a foreign land. Even there, people asked him about the strange letters on his forehead. He wandered restlessly and eventually, unable to bear the stigma, took his own life.

The other brother took a different approach. He said to himself, "I can't run away from the fact that I stole sheep. But I will stay here and win back the respect of my neighbors and myself."

As the years passed, he built a reputation for integrity. One day a stranger saw the old man with the letters branded on his forehead. He asked a citizen of the town what the letters stood for. The villager replied, "It happened a great while ago. I've forgotten the particulars, but I think the letters are an abbreviation of Saint."

You may get away with an evil deed and not be branded for it visibly, but evil deeds always brand your heart. The only true way to change a brand on the heart is to repent and say, "I'm sorry." Then your subsequent acts of kindness can rebuild your good reputation.

Waste no more time arguing what a good man should be.
Be one.

Be an example (pattern) for the
believers, in speech, in conduct,
in love, in faith and in purity.

1 Timothy 4:12 AMP

Although "thermostat" and "thermometer" are close in spelling, there's a world of difference between them.

A thermometer tells you the temperature—whether it's cold or hot—but it does nothing about the situation it identifies. Many people are like thermometers. They readily say, "The church is unfriendly, the town is unreceptive, and the nation is sinful." They describe the atmosphere of a person, place, or institution as being "cold" or "hot." But they do little to change the situation.

Fortunately, other people are like thermostats. When a thermostat senses a room is cold, it quickly and quietly starts the machinery necessary to bring the cold room to an acceptable temperature. If a room is hot, a thermostat cues the system that cools the room.

If you don't like a situation that you face today—whether at home, work, in your community, or in your church—choose to be a thermostat instead of just a thermometer. Make a difference that can "warm things up" or "cool things off" for the comfort of everyone.

Protect your own credibility. One of the highest accolades is the comment, "If he says so, you can bank on it."

Righteous lips are the delight of kings;
and they love him that speaketh right.

Proverbs 16:13

An elderly Southerner walked into his banker's office one day. The banker greeted him warmly and then asked, "What can I do for you?"

The Southerner, who was a typical gentleman from the "old school" replied, "Well, about 35 years ago I loaned a man down South some money—not a very big sum. I told him that whenever I needed it I would let him know and he could repay me. The time has come when I need some money, so I would like to let him know. I would like to have you conduct the transaction for me."

The banker said, "My good friend, you have no claim on that money. The statute of limitations has run against that loan years and years ago."

"Sir," the Southerner replied, "the man to whom I loaned that money is a gentleman. The statute of limitations never runs out for a gentleman."

Sure enough, when the banker made a formal request for the money, it came in a reasonable time! With it was a note: "Thank you. I hope I have the privilege of returning the favor some day."

True Christian character does not seek to escape from a promise. Rather, it reflects our Master whose Word to us is always reliable and never changing.

The man who is born with a talent which he was meant to use finds his greatest happiness in using it.

*But life is worth nothing unless
I use it for doing the work assigned
me by the Lord Jesus.*

Acts 20:24 TLB

When the great golfer Babe Didrikson Zaharias was dying of cancer, her husband, George Zaharias, came to her bedside. Although he desired to be strong for her sake, he found he was unable to control his emotions and began to cry. Babe said to him gently, "Now honey, don't take on so. While I've been in the hospital, I have learned one thing. A moment of happiness is a lifetime, and I have had a lot of happiness."

Happiness does not come wrapped in brightly colored packages as a "gift" given to us by others. Happiness comes when we uncover the gifts that lie within us and begin to use them to please God and bless others.

Happiness flows from within. It is found in the moments of life we label as "quality" rather than quantity. It rises up in life's greatest tragedies when we choose to smile at what we know to be good and lasting, rather than to cry at what temporarily hurts us. George Bernard Shaw once said, "This is the true joy in life: Being used for a purpose recognized by yourself as a mighty one....being a force of nature instead of a feverish, selfish, little clod of ailments and grievances, complaining that the world will not devote itself to making you happy."

A man is not finished when he is defeated. He is finished when he quits.

And let us not be weary in well doing: for in due season we shall reap, if we faint not.

Galatians 6:9

*M*ichael Jordan may not be the greatest basketball player who has ever played the game, but there are countless critics and fans alike who believe he is. It's difficult to think that the Chicago Bulls superstar guard was ever anything but a standout. And yet, Jordan was cut as a sophomore from his high school basketball team. He has said, "The day the cut list was going up, a friend—Leroy Smith—and I went to the gym to look together. If your name was on the list, you made the team. Leroy's name was there, and mine wasn't. I went through the day numb. After school, I hurried home, closed the door to my room and cried so hard." Jordan may not have made the team, but he didn't quit.

At the end of the regular season, he worked up his nerve to ask the coach if he could ride on the bus with the team to the district tournament. The coach agreed...but only if Jordan would carry the players' uniforms. So that's what he did! The following summer, Jordan practiced diligently every day. The next year he made the varsity team, and went on to the University of North Carolina. In his freshman year, his team won the NCAA championship and he was on his way...big time.

If a task is once
begun, never leave
it till it's done.
Be the labor great
or small, do it well
or not at all.

*Whatever your hand finds
to do, do it with your might.*

Ecclesiastes 9:10 NKJV

During the 1984 Summer Olympics, a young American distance runner, Derrick Redmond, was running in front of the pack, well on his way to winning his race. Suddenly, with only a lap to go, Derrick's hamstring muscle snapped. He fell to the ground in agony and fellow runners dodged past him. His parents and friends let out a collective groan, as did millions of Americans who were watching by satellite.

Then, obviously in great pain, Derrick rose from the track and began hopping on one leg toward the finish line. Late stragglers passed him. People on the sidelines who feared for his health yelled for him to lie down. Yet Derrick hopped on. Long after the race was over, Derrick Redmond kept hopping.

Derrick had about 100 yards to go when a figure in the stands began jumping over people, chairs, and then the retaining wall. It was his father, Jim. Rushing to his son's side, he placed his arm around Derrick's waist. Derrick slung his arm over his dad's shoulder and together they half-bounced, half-ran the rest of the way. Derrick didn't wear a gold medal that day, but all who saw him and his father knew...Derrick and Jim Redmond had hearts of gold.

Honor awaits those who *finish* the race.

Give me a stock clerk *with* a goal, and I will give you a man who will make history. Give me a man *without* a goal, and I will give a stock clerk.

■ ■ ■

...fixing our eyes on Jesus...who for the joy set before Him endured the cross, ...and has sat down at the right hand of the throne of God.

Hebrews 12:2 NASB

*S*ome of the world's greatest achievers have been saddled with disabilities and adversities.

Sir Walter Scott...was crippled.

John Bunyan...was imprisoned.

George Washington...was snowbound and freezing in Valley Forge.

Abraham Lincoln...was raised in abject poverty.

Benjamin Disraeli...was subject to bitter religious prejudice.

Franklin D. Roosevelt...was struck down with infantile paralysis.

Ludwig von Beethoven...became deaf.

Glenn Cunningham, a world-record-holding sprinter ...had legs badly burned in a school fire.

Booker T. Washington, Harriet Tubman, Marian Anderson, and George Washington Carver...were all born into a society filled with racial discrimination.

Enrico Caruso...was the first child to survive in a poor Italian family of eighteen children.

Itzhak Perlman, concert violinist...was paralyzed from the waist down at age four.

The vast majority of good excuses for failure...do not exist!

The man who makes no mistakes does not normally make anything.

■ ■ ■

Though he fall, he shall not be utterly cast down: for the Lord upholdeth him with his hand.

Psalm 37:24

When Colin Powell was a young infantry officer, he served in Frankfurt, Germany. One day his platoon was assigned to guard a 280-millimeter atomic cannon. Powell alerted his men, loaded his .45-caliber pistol, and jumped into his jeep. Before he had gone far, he realized that his .45 was gone. Knowing well that losing a weapon is considered serious business, he reluctantly radioed his Captain, Tom Miller.

When Powell returned, Captain Miller said, "I've got something for you" and handed Powell his pistol. He said, "Some kids in the village found it where it fell out of your holster." Powell felt a cold chill. *Kids* had found it? "Yeah," Miller continued, "Luckily they only got off one round before we heard the shot and took the gun away." He concluded, "For God's sake, son, don't let that happen again."

Powell later checked his gun and discovered it had not been fired. He had dropped it in his tent. Miller had fabricated the story to give him a scare.

Concluded Powell, "His example of intelligent leadership was not lost on me. Nobody ever got to the top without slipping up. When someone stumbles, I don't believe in stomping on him. My philosophy is: pick 'em up, dust 'em off, and get 'em moving again."[12]

References

Unless otherwise indicated, all Scripture quotations are taken from the *King James Version* of the Bible.

Scripture quotations marked NIV are taken from the *Holy Bible, New International Version®* NIV®. Copyright © 1973, 1978, 1984 by International Bible Society. Used by permission of Zondervan Publishing House. All rights reserved.

Scripture quotations marked AMP are taken from *The Amplified Bible, Old Testament* copyright © 1965 by Zondervan Publishing House, Grand Rapids, Michigan. *New Testament* copyright © 1958 by The Lockman Foundation, La Habra, California. Used by permission.

Verses marked TLB are taken from *The Living Bible,* copyright © 1971. Used by permission of Tyndale House Publishers, Inc., Wheaton, Illinois 60189. All rights reserved.

Scripture quotations marked NASB are taken from the *New American Standard Bible.* Copyright © The Lockman Foundation 1960, 1962, 1963, 1968, 1971, 1972, 1973, 1975, 1977. Used by permission.

Scripture quotations marked NRSV are taken from *The New Revised Standard Version Bible*, copyright © 1989 by the Division of Christian Education of the Churches of Christ in the United States of America and is used by permission.

Scripture quotations marked NKJV are taken from *The New King James Version* of the Bible. Copyright © 1979, 1980, 1982, 1994 by Thomas Nelson, Inc., Publishers. Used by permission.

Acknowledgements

Elbert Hubbard (12), Robert Schuller (14), Abraham Lincoln (18), A.W. Tozer (20), Dwight L. Moody (22,28,50,88,260), Martin Luther King, Jr. (24), Mark Twain (26,202), Robert Green Ingersol (30), Caroline Fry (34), Thomas Jefferson (36,138), Mike Murdock (38), Paul Tillich (40), Calvin Coolidge (42,92), Frank Crane (44), Cecil G. Osborne (46), David Schwartz (48), James Oliver (54), Anne Bradstreet (56), H.E. Jansen (60), Robert South (64), Margaret Fuller (66), Henry Ward Beecher (68,80), John Wooden (70), James Oppenheim (76), Doris Mortman (82), Richard Exley (86,216), Syrus (90,182), Bill Copland (94), Henry Emerson Fosdick (96), Dr. Eugene Swearingen (98), Ed Cole (100,110), Roy Disney (116), Matthew Prior (118), William A. Ward (120), Moliere (124), Descartes (126), Solon (128), Charles C. Noble (130), Eleanor Roosevelt (132), John Sculley (134), Henry Wadsworth Longfellow (136), Ralph Waldo Emerson (140,264), Charles H. Spurgeon (142), Benjamin Franklin (144), Pauline H. Peters (150), Andrew Jackson (152), Jean Paul Richter (154), William James (156), H.P. Liddon (158),

George Elliott (160), John R. Rice (162), Thomas A. Edison (164), George Edward Woodberry (166), Woodrow Wilson (168), William H. Danforth (172), Lillian Dickson (174), Denis Diderot (176), Earl Nightingale (178), Louis D. Brandeis (180), Roy L. Smith (184), Oliver Wendell Holmes (186,208), Albert Einstein (190), Francis Bacon (194), Zig Ziglar (196), Builder (198), Aristotle (200), George Dana Boardman (204), Gary Smalley & John Trent (206), Arnold H. Glasgow (210), Freeman (212), Doug Larsen (214), Norman Vincent Peale (220), Larry Eisenberg (222), Sir John Buchan (Lord Tweedsmuir) (224), Bern Williams (226), Andrew Carnegie (228), Winston Churchill (240), Jim Patrick (250), Tillotson (252), Billy Graham (254), Parkes Robinson (258), Freidrich Wilhelm Nietzsche (268), James Huxley (270), Aeschylus (272), Gordon van Sauter (276), Lucius Annaeus Seneca (278), George Herbert Palmer (280), Lawrence D. Bell (282), Maurcel Pagnol (284), Euripides (288), H.L. Menken (294), Marcus Aurelius (296), James L Hayes (298), Richard M. Nixon (302), J.C. Penney (306), Edward John Phelps (308).

Endnotes

[1]"How To Grow And Cultivate An Ulcer," rewritten from *Encyclopedia of 7700 Illustrations*, Paul Lee Tan, ed. (Garland, TX: Bible Communications, Inc., 1979), pp. 1449-1450.

[2]*Discipleship Journal*, by Stephen Sorenson, quoted from *Illustrations for Preaching and Teaching*, Craig Brian Larson, ed. (Grand Rapids, MI: Baker Books, 1993), p. 162.

[3]*A Slow and Certain Light*, by Elizabeth Elliot (Dallas, TX: Word Publishing, 1973), p. 19-20.

[4] "The Laggard's Excuse," quoted from *Speaker's Encyclopedia of Stories, Quotations, and Anecdotes*, by Jacob M. Braude (Englewood Cliffs, NJ: Prentice-Hall, 1955), pp. 234-235.

[5]*The Pursuit of Excellence*, by Ted W. Engstrom (Grand Rapids, MI: Zondervan, 1982), pp. 38-39.

[6]"Thank God For You," by Joseph Clark, quoted in *Encyclopedia of 7700 Illustrations*, Paul Lee Tan, ed. (Garland, TX: Bible Communications, Inc., 1979), pp. 462-463.

[7]*Holocaust*, by Gerald Green (New York, NY: Bantam Books, 1978), retold from pp. 132-133.

[8]"I'd Rather See A Sermon," by Edgar A. Guest, quoted in *Encyclopedia of 7700 Illustrations*, Paul Lee Tan, ed. (Garland, TX: Bible Communications, Inc., 1979), p. 1136.

[9]*Up from Slavery* , by Booker T. Washington (New York, NY: Dell Publishing Co., 1965), pp. 23-24.

[10]Poem by Earl Reum quoted in *Speaker's Sourcebook*, by Glenn Van Ekeren (Englewood Cliffs, NJ: Prentice-Hall, 1988), p. 243.

[11]*Newsweek*, March 6, 1995, p. 59.

[12]*My American Journey*, Colin L. Powell, (New York, NY: Random House, 1995) pp. 45-46.

Dear Reader:
If you would like to share some of your favorite quotes on the subject of *manhood*, we would love to hear from you. Our address is:

Honor Books
P.O. Box 55388, Dept. J
Tulsa, Oklahoma 74155

Additional copies of this book and other
titles in the *God's Little Devotional Book* series
are available at your local bookstore.

God's Little Devotional Book
God's Little Devotional Book for Dads
God's Little Devotional Book for Moms
God's Little Devotional Book for Graduates
God's Little Devotional Book for Students
God's Little Devotional Book for Women

HB
HONOR
BOOKS

P.O. Box 55388
Tulsa, Oklahoma 74155

Additional copies of this book and other
titles in the *God's Little Devotional Book* series
are available at your local bookstore.

God's Little Devotional Book
God's Little Devotional Book for Dads
God's Little Devotional Book for Moms
God's Little Devotional Book for Graduates
God's Little Devotional Book for Students
God's Little Devotional Book for Women

P.O. Box 55388
Tulsa, Oklahoma 74155